FARMED OUT

IN

ONTONAGON COUNTY

PAT WINTON

FARMED OUT

IN

ONTONAGON COUNTY

ERNIE
ENJOY

Pat Winton

10/26/24

THIS BOOK IS DEDICATED to my dear wife, Elaine M. Winton, who went to be with the Lord in February of 2024. Her enduring love, infectious smile, inspiration, encouragement, and support provided the drive for me to complete this story of my early life. We loved and enjoyed sixty-two years of married life together, while raising three fantastic children. We were blessed with the addition of two daughters-in-law and a son-in-law, who presented us with seven grandchildren. They have been true blessings from our Lord.

A coming-of-age story of a boy who faced a parent's death, abuse, abandonment, and extreme poverty in a Finnish community within Michigan's Upper Peninsula during the 1940s and 1950s—and how he overcame all odds.

Content Type: Black & White

ISBN/SKU: 9798989948406

ISBN 979-8-9899484-0-6

Acknowledgements

CYNTHIA FURLONG REYNOLDS, author and award-winning journalist, has published twenty-four books and countless articles during her career. I joined her writers' group, THE CEDAR CHIPS, in Dexter, Michigan in 2023, to fulfill a life-long ambition. Cynthia and her fantastic group of writers inspired me to publish this book. Their years of experience, critiques, reviews, humor, and consistent support made this a wonderful journey.

JORDON STYRK, owner of Postal + Prints in Dexter, has assisted me in the preparation for publication with his ideas, technical support, and knowledge of software and printing capabilities.

ANANIYAH.ahmed, 99designs byVista, transformed my ideas for the cover design into reality.

My Biblical inspiration remains ROMANS 8: 31:

What then shall we say to these things? If God is for us, who is against us?

CHAPTERS

PREFACE

I AM WRITING the story of my early life to share my challenging journey into adulthood. A normal, happy family life ended when I was seven and my father died. From that point on, I was the man of the house. But when hard times quickly came, I was farmed out within Michigan's Finnish community in the Upper Peninsula to a series of neighbors and relatives in different locations and environments, some of them abusive. The tales of these episodes and the people remembered aren't meant to be negative or to disparage any persons. They were part of these life experiences.

My normal, fantastic family life ended when I was seven years old, on December 8, 1946. It was a Sunday evening, and my father, mother, sister, and I had just finished dinner. The grownups continued their conversations, but "Blondie and Dagwood" came on the radio at 6:00, and I asked to be excused to go and listen. As I got up, my father gasped and cried, "My God, what has happened?" He fell to the floor and tried to speak.

I ran into the living room to reach the phone, and upon picking up the receiver, I heard the operator ask what number I wanted to call. I screamed, "My father's dying! We need help!" I had been taught our address on the Rockland Road and I gave it to her, but she kept asking for an adult.

In desperation, I hung the phone up and took off running to the neighbors, about one hundred yards up the road. It was a cold, dark December winter night in the Upper Peninsula of Michigan. I ran as fast as I could through the new fallen snow, without a coat or boots, and banged on the neighbors' door. When Mr. Csmarich came to the door, I told him what was happening and how I wasn't able to call for help. Mrs. Csmarich ran to call for an ambulance while her husband and I ran to our house.

My dad died that evening. Before Mr. Csmarich left, he placed his hand on my shoulder and said, "Son, you are now the man of this house."

Those words and this event changed our lives—and from that point on, I tried to live up to that expectation.

More specifically, my father's death changed each life in its own way. My mother was twenty-seven, and my sister was four. We had no life insurance or any money.

Eventually, my mother sold the house, and we went on Social Security. As I recall, my sister and I each received sixteen dollars a month and our mother twenty-five. We were fortunate to have a debt-free ten-year-old 1936 Chevrolet Coupe, with a rumble seat. We kept it in running condition for the next four years.

I had been told I was now the man of the family, and you can be certain that I assumed that role.

I believe in Jesus Christ. From the age of eleven, I have asked Him to lead me. There have been straying times, but in total, I have tried to follow His lead.

You will note throughout these chapters of my life that people in and outside of my family intervened in my life exactly when I most needed help and guidance. I give these people recognition for the fact that God brought them into my life and helped me to prevail. I'm also thankful to have grown up in America, the greatest and best place in the world, a place where a strong work ethic and a strong foundation can help anyone achieve success.

I learned that hard work and perseverance can—and will—pay off, and I hope these stories will demonstrate that success can be achieved and adversities can be overcome.

Origins

In order for you to better understand my story, I need to describe the background of my origin and early beginnings.

My mother's parents each independently emigrated to the United States from Finland as young individuals, to avoid the Russian czar's 1881 edicts imposed on the Finnish people. At that time, Finland was under the control of Russia, and the czar demanded that Russian become the official language and young Finnish men would be conscripted into the Russian Army. Essentially all Finnish national feelings were being stamped out. These Russian edicts didn't end until about 1918, with the Russian Revolution.

Andrew (Antti) Hietala from Oulu, Finland, was born in 1874, and emigrated about 1900. After extensive study, I wasn't able to find any records of how he arrived in America. According to the family story, he had been a Russian soldier, and was naturalized as an American citizen somewhere out West. He somehow ended up in the Copper Country of Upper Michigan—that story was lost.

Kreeta Kukkola from Ii (pronounced "E"), Finland was born in 1874. In 1899, she sailed from Helsinki and landed in Boston. How she ended up in the Copper Country of Upper Michigan is also unknown, but I do know that many Finnish people arrived in the Copper Country because the terrain, forests, seasons, work and living opportunities made them feel like they were home. This was often discussed when I lived in Ontonagon County.

Antti and Kreeta were married in 1901, in Ishpeming, Michigan, and homesteaded in Ontonagon County on eighty acres in Interior Township. This was a time when much of the virgin timber had been logged off in Ontonagon County, and the land was opened to homesteading.

Their farm was two and a half miles west of Trout Creek (pronounced "crik."). The Trout Creek ran through the town of about five hundred people, with a large saw mill there employing many men. Beginning in 1887, the railroad was completed and ran through the town, providing transportation for lumber out and logs into the mill, as well as food and farming supplies to the stores. Passenger service was also provided. Small schools were scattered through the countryside; the consolidation process for schools began in 1930.

Nine children were born to Antti and Kreeta. My mother, Signe Irene Hietala, always called Irene, was the youngest. She was born in Trout Creek in March of 1919. Both of her parents died in 1932, only two months apart, Kreeta from a brain hemorrhage and Antti from stomach cancer. The oldest son, Jack, was thirty years old when his parents died, but he wasn't able to keep the farm operation going. Life on a farm was dangerous, and Jack had been kicked in the head by a horse. He was confined to the Mental Institution in Newberry when his parents passed.

The only other son, Andrew, was fourteen years old when he lost his parents, and he was sent to an Army Civilian Conservation Corps camp in 1934. Because no one was available to continue the farming operations, the farm was abandoned, but the taxes were paid by someone in the Hietala family, to keep the property in the family.

All I know about my mother's early life is that she was farmed out to two older sisters' homes in Ontonagon. She was only able to finish the eighth grade in the rural schools located at the crossroads area called Agate, one mile west of the homestead. Neither of her older sisters sent her to high school in Ontonagon, so she went to work in a nearby hotel, cleaning and doing laundry.

My mother was a beautiful, slender woman, about five-foot-seven inches tall, with dark brown hair and beautiful eyes. As I recall, my dad was one inch shorter, and they often kidded each other about the height difference. With only an eighth-grade education, my mother spoke and wrote fluently in both Finnish and English. She was extremely intelligent, a Christ believer, and she wrote with precise cursive writing, which she demonstrated throughout her life.

Dad understood some of the Finnish language, but didn't speak it. Mother would laugh at his attempts.

The Winton family began in the New World as Puritans, with the arrival of John Winton into the New Haven Colony in 1640. We don't know his hometown. Nathan Winton, the great-great-grandson of John Winton, served in the Continental Army during the American Revolution under General Washington, including time at Valley Forge.

After the Revolution, Nathan moved from Connecticut to Crawford County, Pennsylvania, and went into the timbering business. Nathan's son Samuel was born in 1789, and married Margaret Coil in 1811. Their son, my great-grandfather, Charles Samuel Winton, was born in 1823, in Centerville, Crawford County.

In 1847, Charles married Phebe Waid, a local girl born in 1826, in Crawford County. They had ten children. At some point—I don't know when—Charles and Phebe moved from Pennsylvania to Brown County, Wisconsin, to go into the timber business. By the time their son Ralph was born in 1856, they were living in Wisconsin. My grandfather, Wilbur P. Winton, was born in 1864, in DePere, Brown County. Wilbur and his father Charles eventually established logging operations in northern Wisconsin and in Iron and Gogebic Counties in Michigan during the 1880s.

In 1897, Wilbur P married his first wife, Hattie Thompson, who came from Green Bay, in Oconto, Wisconsin. The Winton family neither spoke of, nor answered questions about, Hattie. I don't know anything about her or their three sons (Guy Wade, Jay C, and Walter Ralph). I do know that they lived on the original homestead in Bates Township, Iron County, Michigan, near the town of Iron River.

Since this was new territory, First Generation people (most likely Chippewa) lived in the area and regularly visited the Winton homestead. Stories indicate that Hattie would awake in the morning and find Indian people sleeping on the floor of her kitchen. She couldn't accept this open-door living situation, and she decided to leave. At a time when divorce was unusual, Wilbur P and Hattie were divorced, and Wilbur P was left to raise the three young sons.

Wilbur hired a number of women cooks to prepare meals for his logging camps, one of them Anna Dorthea Schacht. She became his second wife. They raised Wilbur P's first three sons and had three children of their own: Wilbur J, Ethel, and Ralph.

My father, Wilbur J, was born in Oconto Falls in 1900, and I remember him telling me that he only went through the fourth grade. He also told me he began working at nine years of age in his father's lumber camps, taking care of the horses and driving them to move timber. Wilbur J married a local girl, Bertha Rechel, in 1918, and they had four sons (Lester, Earl, Lloyd, and James (Hank). Once again, the family never spoke about why Wilbur J and Bertha separated in 1938. However, Bertha assumed care of the four sons and remarried as soon as the divorce was final.

Wilbur J carried on the Winton tradition of timbering in Michigan's Iron and Gogebic counties of Michigan, working with his father until Wilbur P died in 1925. In time, the timber areas were logged out, and Wilbur J established a heavy-equipment dealership, which closed during the Depression. Then he became a sales manager for the Drott Tractor Co., selling heavy equipment throughout northern Minnesota, Wisconsin, and the Upper Peninsula.

My parents met in Ontonagon and fell in love. I don't know how or exactly when they met or what transpired in their time together. No information was given to me or to my sister, Trish. I do know they left for Houston, Texas, in 1939, while waiting for Wilbur J's divorce to be finalized. I was born May 29, 1939, in St. Louis, Missouri.

Early Memories

Mother told me that I was getting ready to enter the world on their trip south, so they stopped in St. Louis, where Mother's older sister Lillian and her husband, Leo Jones, lived. When I was ready to travel, we departed for Houston, where Dad and Mother married after Dad's divorce was finalized. My dear sister, Patricia (Trish) Irene Winton, was born in Houston in February of 1942. I now had a sister! And the oldest three Winton boys (Lester, Earl, and Lloyd) stayed close to their biological father, my Dad. Lester even visited us in Houston, with his wife, Norma, and son, Gerry. Earl and Lloyd both served in WWII, so there was no opportunity for them to visit during our time in Houston.

I remember life as being great in our 105 South 70th Street duplex near Buffalo Bayou, even though we had little money. Based on pictures and a little memory on my part, we were a happy family. I remember a day when Dad didn't come home at his usual time, and Mother became desperate and very worried. It was very late in the evening when he returned, and I was still up, keeping Mother company. Dad was very tired.

He told us he had been arrested and taken to jail. He described how he was in a traffic jam, and a police officer repeatedly yelled at him to move his car forward, closer to the car in front. Finally, the police officer got right in his face and Dad said, "Do I go over the car or under it?" I don't remember if other words were spoken, but I know Dad was one tough person. He was taken to jail, and was finally released that evening.

Dad operated bulldozing equipment all during WWII, preparing air fields for the Army outside Houston. But we all returned to Ontonagon in early 1944. Dad and Mother bought a beautiful two-story house on Rockland Road, across from the Catholic cemetery. Dad and his business partners, (unknown to me) from Iron River set up a company selling the operational use of their equipment, to make logging roads in the western part of the Upper Peninsula. As sales manager, Dad searched for loggers who needed assistance getting timber out of the woods. Dad drove a pickup with a large diesel tank that kept the bulldozers running with diesel fuel.

Dad almost always had a lowboy tractor and trailer in our drive next to the garden, ready to move the heavy equipment to a new job. He often took me with him. I spent many weekend hours in the lowboy tractor trailer or the pickup, visiting lumber camps. I also rode on bulldozers actually making logging roads.

The logging camps were full of men of many nationalities, and many didn't speak English well. At an early age, I learned a logging camp rule: when at the meal table, no talking was allowed. Words spoken, or attempted to be spoken in English, often offended someone, and this would generate a fight. So, Dad taught me not to say a word at the logging camp meal table.

One day early on—I was most likely seven years old—we were having lunch at a lumber camp. I was positioned across from Dad at a long picnic table, in what today would be called a mess hall, with lumberjacks on each side of us. Whenever a plate of food went by me, the lumberjacks near me would load my plate. Thick black coffee in a large white mug was placed in front of me by a lady cook. As I reached for the metal-topped glass container with a hole in it, Dad shook his head. I couldn't stand strong coffee, so I reached again, thinking I'd help myself to some sugar.

Dad's head now shook much harder, and a stern look followed. I had no choice. I didn't drink the coffee. As we walked

18

out of the mess hall, he grabbed me by the shoulder and said, "You should know by now that was salt. There's never sugar on the table in a lumber camp."

When I was six or seven, my mother, father, sister, and I went swimming in Lake Superior at the Ontonagon Community Park. It was a beautiful day, sun shining brightly and just a slight westerly breeze keeping the flies off the beach.

Lake Superior was cold, but not unbearable. My father informed me that there was a severe drop-off a short distance from shore and I mustn't go out very far. The waves were about a foot high, and I enjoyed running into them. I found a large log on the shore, pushed it into the lake, and began riding on it. The waves gave me a great ride. As I remember, I was on the log when a wave took me out farther than I expected. The log rolled, and I went under. I couldn't feel the bottom of the lake. I remember looking up, seeing the log high above me.

I don't remember my father pulling me out, but I think I swallowed the lake. Dad and Mother said I came very close to drowning. I believe the Big Lady—the name used by Upper Peninsula natives for Lake Superior—and God gave me more time to be here on earth.

CHAPTER ONE

Life Without Father

AFTER MY FATHER died, Mother had to make decisions about our future. I recall that Dad's first sons wanted her to move to Iron River, Michigan, where they all lived, but she very quickly said no. Another option was to sell the big house and stay in Ontonagon. The two sisters she had lived with as a girl after their parents died still lived there. Again, she refused, as she didn't want to stay where Dad had died.

The eighty-acre Hietala homestead in Trout Creek had been passed on to Aunt Lydia, mother's sister, and her husband Bruno Helsius. They decided to give a small parcel of the Hietala land to Mother, so she could live near them and her other sister and brother-in-law, Naima and Victor Aho. With the money from selling the house in Ontonagon and assistance from family and friends, the "little house" was constructed in 1947, on the original Hietala homestead.

The house had two tiny bedrooms, a kitchen, and living room. A fuel oil heater in the living room and a small wood stove in the kitchen were the sources of heat and food preparation. Electricity was not initially available, but lines were strung in late 1948. With electricity, we were in heaven.

We obtained our water from the neighbors' well. It was much closer to the little house than Lydia and Bruno's well, which did not have an outside hand pump. Trish and I were assigned to obtain water. We had to pump water into containers and transport them home using our little red wagon in summer and a toboggan in winter. The outhouse was situated behind the house.

Although Ontonagon County is the second largest in the State of Michigan in acreage, it had (and mostly likely still has) the second smallest population per square mile. I once saw a figure from the 1950s that said the county had just over one person per square mile. In 2021, the population was still less than two people per square mile. In 1947, there were very few companies or businesses in the county, and even fewer in the Interior Township area, resulting in few job opportunities for Mother.

After settling into our new little house, Mother began suffering severe back difficulties. She was sent to the Ontonagon Hospital on many occasions, and she would be gone for days each time. This situation continually created challenges for us all: where we could live and who would care for Trish, my beautiful blond sister, and me.

Our farming-out days began.

Trish was usually farmed out to the Ollilas, our neighbors who provided our water. John Ollila was a school teacher in Trout Creek, so he would take Trish to school and bring her back. Gertrude Ollila was always at home, so if there was no school, Trish was always cared for.

I was the problem for Mother. Sometimes I was welcomed at Aunt Lydia's house, which was next door, but only for meals. Before I was nine, I had to sleep alone at home, since their house was small and my aunt didn't have a place for me to sleep. At least I was able to catch the bus to and from school.

The other alternative was for me to be farmed out with Aunt Naima and Uncle Vic. When I was there, I had to sleep in the attic, do chores, and walk to school, which was about a mile and a half away. The meals were great, as Naima's cooking was so much better than Lydia's.

Finally, Mother was sent to Ann Arbor for surgery on her back. She was gone three months, followed by weeks of recovery. This way of life, being constantly farmed out, went on for two years, from 1947 to mid-1949. Trish and I were unable to maintain a close relationship because we never had time together, though our fondness for each other never changed. We could only see each other when in school, so we therefore grew apart in many ways.

From the night my father died, my order of the day was to find a way to gain income. Even at eight, I tried to earn some money to help Mother. One of the men courting my mother hired me to drive his tractor in his hay field when I was eight years old. I quickly learned to drive, and he paid Mother for my help. When she was well, Mother was always asking neighbors and friends if there was something she could do for income. An excellent baker, she started to bake and sell baked goods, especially chiffon cakes for special events, using her small wood-burning kitchen stove.

Every cake was a major investment of ingredients, and as I recall, her recipe required about a dozen egg whites and a precise oven temperature. She knew how to select the size and type of wood, and just where to place it in the firebox to keep a precise oven temperature. The cakes were beautiful and she had quite a reputation for excellent chiffon cakes. One fateful day, I came into the kitchen, via the back door, and slammed the door shut. I heard a very loud scream. Mother had opened the oven door at that moment, and the slamming door resulted in a very flat chiffon cake. It had been destined for a wedding reception.

Not only was another cake required, the time was short and an investment of another dozen eggs would be necessary—a total disaster. We both cried, my cries due to a sore bottom.

Living in the Upper Peninsula countryside certainly had its negatives and positives. The abundance of wildlife opened opportunities to earn money. At first, my main effort was trapping weasels. By the time I was eight, I was already successful. I ran a trap line in the neighbor's woods and fields since my cousin Marvin Helsius set his traps in the homestead woods and fields.

I skinned and dried the hides, and sent the perfect hides to St. Louis, Missouri, where I was able to receive the maximum price per hide: one dollar for a small weasel pelt, and up to two dollars and fifty cents for a large one. The hides had to be in good shape and all white, which meant they had to be trapped in the winter, when weasels turn white. I continued to trap, even when I was farmed out, until I left home and moved to Ontonagon at the start of tenth grade.

One special moment took place in the 1948 summer, when Mother, Trish, and I drove to Ontonagon with the War Bond that my father had bought for me. I used this bond to purchase a new red Schwinn bicycle. But disaster soon followed. On my first day learning to ride, I ran into a tree. The shiny front fender was pushed back into the frame and dented. A nine-year-old boy cried that day. That dent was still in the fender when I left it on the farm in 1954.

Opportunities to earn money came in other ways. I learned that if I agreed to purchase a box of six metal containers of Bolen Salve, I could resell them for a profit. This salve was used to draw out infections from the body. It had to be melted and then placed on a cut or splinter when it was hot. After the salve was left on for a number of days, the infection would be drawn out.

I could see myself as a salesman, selling this salve to grateful farmers and woodsmen, who were always dealing with splinters, cuts, and infections. Anticipating great success, I borrowed money from my mother and purchased the first order. I then attempted to sell the six cans of salve.

I rode my bike from farm to farm, convinced it was a sure-fire investment. In the end, we piled a number of the cans of this salve in our medicine cabinet.

My dream of becoming a super salesman was dashed.

During the summer when trout season was open, I fished for brook trout as often as possible, to help reduce the grocery bill. My fish pole was a government pole (a thin long sapling) with fish line wound around the business end, with fish hook, sinker, and a worm. I worked the stream on the homestead farm and continued downstream to an area where the clay banks of the creek caused the clear water to turn brown. I knew all the holes and would proudly bring home a mess of brook trout sufficient for a meal for our family.

Trout Creek was an appropriate name for the small town two and a half miles east of our house. The creek flowed through the east side of town on its northerly path to join the Middle Branch of the Ontonagon River, and then flowed on to Lake Superior. A dam had been made on the south side of town near the sawmill, to create the Mill Pond, which was used by the Abbot Fox Sawmill for floating logs. The creek entrance of the pond was a great place for catching trout.

As every boy at that time knew, floating the logs removed the dirt from their exterior. The cleaned logs were then passed on to the Hot Pond, next to the sawmill, where hot water and steam removed, or at least loosened, the bark before the logs were cut into boards. A large steam-generating plant cut away the bark before the saw-cutting operation. The unused steam and water were then returned to the Hot Pond. My Uncle Bruno was running the sawmill steam plant when we moved to Trout Creek in 1947, and he continued there until the mill was closed in the 1960s.

Trout Creek, upstream from the mill pond, was an excellent place to fish for brook trout. In addition, upstream near the head waters, the Department of Natural Resources stocked the creek with rainbow trout. My cousin Marvin and I discovered when this event would most likely take place. I don't recall the source of this information, but I believe it was published in the local paper. We would get there early and watch from a hiding place. After the DNR workers released the trout, we waited, to be certain the men had departed. Then we snuck in and caught our limit of rainbow trout. These new fish in the creek were usually very hungry.

I think the men delivering the fish knew what we were doing, but we were able to continue without bother for a couple of years.

School Days & Fun Nights

Going to school in Trout Creek was a unique experience. I had gone to school in Ontonagon for my kindergarten, first, and second grades, and we had thirty to forty students per class there. In Trout Creek, I had between eight to eighteen classmates per grade, from the third through the ninth grade.

In my second year in Trout Creek, the fourth and fifth grades were joined together with one teacher, Mrs. McLaughlin—a major adjustment for me. The rest of the classes through the ninth grade were larger and taught in separate rooms because of the numbers of children born to veterans returning after the war.

The multi-class environment during these early years of my schooling was very significant to me. I was able to see and hear what was being taught in the next year's class, and I constantly challenged myself to learn what the fifth graders were learning, while still continuing my fourth-grade work.

Living with my Finnish relatives and other Finnish families was extremely challenging, as well as fun. Many of the people, family, and friends, were original immigrants from Finland and spoke little or no English. My mother and other first-generation Finnish mothers didn't want their children to speak with an accent, so we weren't taught Finnish. I consider that a real negative for me, as I wish I had learned to speak the Finnish language fluently.

Every Saturday night was Sauna Night—when we took a Finnish bath in the outdoor wood-heated saunas. When invited, we would go the home of a friend or family member on Saturday night for the ritual. Sometimes another family would also be invited. The host family would heat up the sauna late Saturday afternoon, and at night everyone entered the hosts' sauna in a specific order. The first people in the sauna were the women with young children, usually a maximum of six at a time. The next group consisted of the children, boys and girls together, for a maximum of six. Finally, the sauna was filled with six men and older boys. I didn't understand why I was moved from the boys'-and-girls' group to the men's group when it happened.

After everyone had completed their baths, the host family served coffee and wonderful Finnish baked specialties.

I was challenged when communicating with the adults, many of whom didn't speak English. I found if I spoke very slowly and distinctly, I was able to communicate. That also worked for Mother's Bible Study group. Many of those ladies couldn't read or easily speak English. Mother insisted that Trish and I attend, as there was no one to care for us in the evening. I was often asked to read the Bible, of course in English, since I spoke slowly and distinctly. This habit of speech has remained with me throughout my life and has been a real benefit when communicating in my extensive foreign business dealings. But it was a negative when conversing with fast-speaking Americans.

The Finnish Lutheran Church, Suomi Synod, had three churches in the southern section of the county. The parsonage was located in Trout Creek, but the minister was responsible for providing a sermon in all three churches every Sunday. The first sermon was in Ewen, the second in Painesville, and the third in our church, which was located across the highway and railroad tracks from our little house.

At this time, all the church services were in Finnish, except for one English service at Christmas. Eventually, the number of English services increased, and when I left the area, there was one yearly Finnish service at Christmas.

Mother was asked to be church treasurer, and she took this job very seriously. Part of her responsibility was to pay the preacher in cash each Sunday, after all three church services. On a number of occasions, the combined Sunday collection offerings were insufficient to cover the minister's salary, and, my mother would open her purse and remove enough money to make up the difference.

I will always remember the one time I scolded her for using our few dollars to make up for what others didn't contribute. She calmly rebuked me, and told me that God knew what she was doing, and He would make certain that we were cared for. She was right. I have always remembered this experience and have always made giving to God's work a priority in my life.

By the time I was eight, I was already successful. I ran a trap line in the neighbor's woods and fields.

CHAPTER TWO

FARMED OUT

ONCE WE MOVED to the little house in Trout Creek, Mother certainly became the center of attraction for single men. After all, many of them were returning from serving our country in World War II and were anxious to start their civilian lives. And Mother was such a beautiful young woman at twenty-eight-years of age.

Of course, because she had two young children, some stood back while others showed their interest. After a couple of years, four men were most often in the picture.

The neighbor across the road was single and about her age. He taught me how to drive his tractor when I was eight. He was a nice man, but I thought she could find someone that had more to offer.

Another gentleman was from somewhere near Grand Rapids. A relatively small man, he came to hunt partridge in the fall for at least two years. He was very quiet and nice to Trish and me.

Another local man was a farmer who attended our church. He showed interest, but, from my point of view, he didn't make any effort to date her.

The fourth was an Army veteran from the war in Europe who had recently returned to Trout Creek. He was the son of a prominent Finnish family in Interior Township and attended our church. He was then working as an auto mechanic in Bruce Crossing, a community just west of our house.

Now, the head of the house—me!—spent a lot of time trying to figure out which man might be trying to take over my assignment as head of the house. In the end, I had no say in the decision.

George Henry Kaare was raised in Trout Creek, graduated from Trout Creek High School, went to Suomi College for a time, and served in the Army during World War II. But he was not a nice man. I was extremely worried that he might become the head of the house. George had no children and hadn't even been around children. I had no doubt that he certainly disliked me.

Throughout the time while dating Mother, he frequently complained that I was too fat and she should change who I was. George single-handedly changed who I was.

When they were both thirty-one years old, Mother married George on September 1, 1950. I not only lost my assignment as the man of the house, I wasn't part of the new program.

Trish and I were informed they had worked out a deal for our care while they went to Detroit to work and save money to buy a farm. We were to be farmed out "for probably one to two years." Trish would return to the Ollilas' house, next door to our little house on the homestead. John and Gertrude Ollila didn't have children, but Gertrude was a sweet lady and served as our church pianist. John was a grade-school teacher in Trout Creek. Trish, now in the third grade, would be living in a fine loving home.

I was told I would live with Aunt Naima and Uncle Vic Aho, where I had often stayed when Mother was in the hospital with her frequent back problems. Uncle Vic and Aunt Naima never had children. My uncle made their living working at the local sawmill, fishing, and trapping.

Aunt Naima was less than five feet tall, about one hundred pounds, and had a pleasant personality that showed how much she cared for me. She was an excellent cook and was noted for her high- speed walking. No distance was too far for Aunt Naima, and she certainly believed that walking was good for your health. I knew walking would be part of my daily routine. Probably the walking requirement, her clean house syndrome, and the fact I would have to sleep in the attic convinced me I didn't want to live there for a couple of years.

Their house consisted of a kitchen, living room, one bedroom, a pantry where Uncle Vic's father slept, and the attic for yours truly. Mr. Aho was at least eighty years old and didn't speak English, so we developed a way of grunting and pointing in order to communicate.

My bedroom, the unheated attic, was freezing in winter and roasting in summer. The bed was set on loose boards that also provided a walkway. Small windows were set in the gable ends, and openings under the eaves permitted ventilation. Screens on all the openings were intended to keep the mosquitoes out, but they didn't keep the light snow from blowing up into the attic.

Uncle Vic was about five feet six inches tall, and had a solid muscular body, making him someone you didn't want to mess with. He had been a champion wrestler in his youth and even competitively wrestled in St. Louis. His thumbs had been broken when wrestling, so the thumb joint was actually located farther than normal from the palm, thereby resulting in a pair of huge hands. He was known for his honesty and for being the best trapper in Western Upper Peninsula and an outstanding guide for fishing. Uncle Vic was the barber for all the men and boys of the family. He was famous for using hand clippers and often didn't complete the final squeeze of the clippers to finish the cut, thereby removing hair from the scalp.

His large powerful hands would clamp down on your head, so any movement was impossible. All the while he was cutting your crew cut, with a flat top and straight sides, he would make certain you were reminded, "Kids should be seen and not heard."

Vic worked at the sawmill when there was lumber to be cut, but he really made his living by trapping and guiding people on fishing trips. Coyotes brought a twenty-dollar bounty for a male and a twenty-five-dollar bounty for a female, regardless of age. Timber wolves brought a bounty of fifty dollars, the big money. The bounty for a fox was five dollars, and the hides were worth another ten to twenty dollars.

In November, there was a state-authorized two-week trapping season for mink and muskrat, and in the spring there was another authorized, month-long beaver-trapping season. Mink pelts brought thirty to fifty dollars, muskrats one to two dollars, and beaver thirty to fifty dollars. Fur buyers from Chicago and St. Louis would come to bid and purchase Uncle Vic's furs, as he was well known for having the best pelts in the U.P. I never had the opportunity to be part of the sale of furs, as I was in school when this happened.

I remember coming home from school and finding Vic and Naima celebrating their proceeds with coffee and Finnish biscuit after the buyer left.

Sleeping in the attic was difficult most times of the year, but especially when animals were skinned and the hides left there to dry.

Vic decided to train this kid in the art of making a living by trapping. He had me help him skin and prepare the hides for drying. Later, I had to scrape the fat from the drying hides so he would receive the highest price.

Once, when I was skinning a bobcat that had been assigned to me, I found a spent 38-caliber bullet under the hide at the bobcat's tail. It was the result of the normal way to kill the animal: a single shot between the eyes. That avoided any damage to the pelt.

I kept that bullet for years.

The winter of 1950 was especially tough, with below-zero temperatures—often minus-thirty degrees Fahrenheit and we had more than three hundred inches of snow. Old Mr. Aho did the snow shoveling and chopped and delivered the wood for the kitchen stove. Vic had installed a fuel oil heater in the living room, so they had uniform heat in the living room and adjoining bedroom. The wood-burning kitchen stove would keep the kitchen area and Mr. Aho's room warm for a short time after everyone went to bed. However, there was no heat in the attic.

If the outside wind came from the west and the snow was very fine, I would find a small snow drift on my bed when I woke up in the morning. The memories of trying to get dressed under the huge pile of blankets will remain with me forever. So will the odors of all those hides drying next to my bed.

One morning in the winter of 1950, the temperature dropped to forty-two degrees below zero when I set out to walk to school. Of course, we didn't calibrate the outdoor thermometer, but I can confirm that it showed minus forty-two degrees—and that was cold. I walked the one-and-a-half miles to school, a walk to always remember. Each step in the snow sounded like the crack of a 22 rifle being fired. I was so happy when I could at last climb the stairs to the school, but, alas, the door was locked.

Before me was a little sign attached to the inside glass announcing, "No School Today." The walk back was one of the longest walks I've ever made.

Once in a while, Uncle Vic would invite me to accompany him on his trap line. The first time was the most memorable.

Two years earlier, my Dad's sister, Aunt Ethel, had given me skis for Christmas. They were store-bought, with those little wire binders that could be adjusted to hold your swampers in the toehold. Swampers are boots with leather tops, rubber lowers, and felt inserts. I set off with my store-bought skis. Uncle Vic had his home-made Finnish cross-country skis. They were at least eight feet long and very narrow in the front and back. Those traditional skis were very flexible, so the tip of the skis would always be up and pointed to the top of the snow. When my uncle came to a fallen log, he would step out of the leather strap holding his swampers and step over the log while catching the leather strap with his toe on the other side of the log. Zip, zip, and he was moving on.

Well, can you imagine me making my way in the four-foot blanket of snow, trying to undo the spring binders of each ski, climbing over the log, and re-clamping the swampers. Uncle Vic was very upset with my inability to keep up. I heard words that I can't repeat here.

Finally, we arrived at the Sturgeon River, about four miles from the truck. "My trap is sprung and the coyote has moved downstream," he told me. I hadn't even seen a mark in the snow, let alone realized all this information.

About a mile down the river, Vic said the coyote had crossed the river and we now had to follow it across. Out came his knife, a big Finnish puukko, and he quickly cut a pole. He started across the river with snow-covered ice and open water everywhere, using the pole to check for thin ice, with me following in his tracks. I held my breath and wondered if we would safely arrive on the other side. And then I realized that we would have to make a return trip.

Once we were on the other side of the river, we climbed the steep bank and there sat the coyote we had been following. He was entrapped in a large blackberry bush, the trap attached to his hind leg.

I need to explain that the trap chain is always attached to a small tree trunk, about two feet long, with the branches cut off about one or two inches from the trunk. When caught in the trap, the coyote can drag the wood log and move onward, but the log will eventually get caught in the brush. The coyote is able to move around, but can't free itself. If the trap is attached to an immovable object, the coyote will chew off its leg to get away.

This time, the coyote just sat there with its tail wagging and its ears straight up, looking straight at us. Uncle Vic sternly said, "STOP." We were side by side and about twenty feet away from the coyote when Uncle Vic pulled out his trusty High Standard pistol with a 22-caliber barrel installed. This pistol had a changeable barrel; if Vic went into bear country, it was fitted with the 38-caliber barrel.

"Watch this," Vic said. He moved one step forward toward the coyote, a slide forward on his skis. The coyote lunged for his head. The gun fired. The coyote was shot between the eyes.

I guess I should have mentioned that Vic had fitted me with one of his home-made birch bark barrel backpacks when we left the truck. Well, you can imagine what happened next: he placed the thirty-five-pound coyote in my barrel and we started back to the truck.

I imagine that Uncle Vic sat in the truck for almost an hour before I arrived, just before dark. Upon arrival at home, I removed the coyote's scalp and flesh, as I had been taught, and prepared the scalp so it could be turned in at the Department of Natural Resources office for the bounty. While I was doing this, Uncle Vic was removing the body parts and identifying the sex. From that time on, I was fitted with a pair of Finnish skis, most likely Mr. Aho's, and I could then keep up with Uncle Vic.

CHAPTER THREE

Winter Fun: Ice Skating

IN THE WINTER of 1950, I was eleven years old, a sixth-grade student who had been farmed out when my mother and new stepfather left for Detroit. That year the Trout Creek School decided students should have the opportunity to ice skate during recess.

An adjoining property owner to the south of the school owned land that had an old tennis court. The neighbor agreed to let the school build an ice rink on the old tennis court. It wasn't an ideal situation. The broken concrete of the tennis court was not level, so many areas of concrete were above the rink ice, making for challenging skating. We quickly learned to try to avoid the bad spots, but that was almost impossible, as there were so many areas of visible concrete.

My cousin Glenn, who lived in Ontonagon, had received new skates, and I was given his old ones. I had never skated before, and the skates were a couple or more sizes larger than my feet. Aunt Naima gave me many pairs of Uncle Vic's socks to fill in the extra space.

Many of the town kids had ice rinks in their yards and were excellent skaters. Us rural farm kids certainly didn't have the time or benefit of this luxury. In my class, only a few of the boys were from the farm, so the town guys had the advantage. All of us spoke English, but there were two who spoke Finnish at home.

One afternoon recess, we boys were playing tag. Since I was a very slow runner, the ice skates gave me ability to keep up with the guys. I was even able to avoid being "IT" all the time.

But Roy Tahtinen decided I was the one to chase. I sped away as fast I could. When I looked back, I saw that I was well ahead of him. But I didn't see the bare concrete. I flew through the air. As I was about to hit the ice, I folded and placed my arms ahead of my body to break the unavoidable impact with the ice. Upon landing, not softly, my head was thrown downward. Everyone heard a loud "Bang" as my face hit the ice.

When I came to, I saw, there on the ice, my two front teeth. They had broken off right at the gum.

Since my mother and stepfather were in Detroit, Uncle Vic took me to the Ewen dentist—the only one in the southern part of the county—the next day. It didn't take very long for the dentist to say, "There's nothing I can do for you except to place pegs into the roots and hope." Since we didn't have money for expensive dental work, the roots were left to rot. After a long and painful time, they were finally pulled.

Going without two front teeth was a real challenge for a boy in the sixth grade. This was endured through the seventh, eighth, and part of the ninth grades. Missing my teeth was especially difficult when someone would start singing "All I Want for Christmas is My Two Front Teeth." All I could do was to increase my grade point and work harder in everything I did during these years.

Finally, in my freshman year of high school, my stepfather decided to pay for a partial plate with two teeth that didn't match the color of mine. I had learned to keep my upper lip over the opening and this continues today. Many people ask why I don't smile. This is why.

Now, the head of the house - me! - spent a lot of time trying to figure out which man might be trying to take over my assignment as head of the house.

CHAPTER FOUR

FAMILY FARM YEARS

MOTHER AND GEORGE RETURNED from Detroit in the late summer of 1952, ready to purchase a farm. As soon as George reappeared in my life, the same old treatment and name-calling started up again. Basically no change.

I was actually sorry they returned, although I can now admit that I was very happy to live with my mother and sister. Trish had grown into a different person, though. She seemed distant from all of us and very quiet. Before being farmed out, she was smiley and happy most of the time. I was devastated and sorry to see the changes, but believed she, too, was affected by not having a caring and loving mother when she was eight to ten years old. I worried that she didn't want to be back with us.

We all moved to the new farm in the fall of 1952. George immediately purchased a herd of cattle from a couple in Paines-ville. As I recall, he had ten milk cows and a couple of heifers. So, at the age of thirteen, I was now a new farmer, or at least expected to learn to be one.

The farm covered eighty acres at the end of North Agate Road, about two miles from M-28 and one-half-mile from the nearest neighboring farm. North Agate Road was about four miles west of Trout Creek. Because of the dense woods and ninety-degree turn in the road leading up to the house and barn, no neighbor's buildings could be seen from our farm. The land hadn't been cultivated, by my guess, for least twenty years, and many of the fields were overgrown with brush.

Some of the land was swamp. I estimate that only thirty to forty acres were tillable, and not all together in one area. This poor definition of a farm was totally surrounded by woods located a mile and a half east of the Middle Branch of the Ontonagon River. We were two miles west of farms to the east and twenty miles south of the nearest road to the north.

In other words. We were in the middle of nowhere.

The farm buildings consisted of a fairly new barn, a two-car garage with dirt floor and practically unusable doors, an old horse barn behind the cow barn, and an old sauna whose roof had collapsed into the building. The three-bedroom house needed an unbelievable amount of renovation.

Two small bedrooms upstairs were tucked under sloped ceilings that would only allow someone under six feet to stand in the center. Trish had one, I had the other. The house was heated with a wood stove in the living room and a wood-burning kitchen stove. Water was gravity-fed from a spring on the hillside behind the house.

Gravity-fed water meant no water pumps were needed, but the water flow was painfully slow. We had an indoor toilet and even electricity—marvelous!

The school bus turned around next to the house, so Trish and I wouldn't have to stand outside in the snow or rain waiting for the bus to arrive. In the mornings, we got onto the bus after it picked up all the kids farther out of town. However, on the way home, we were the last to get off the bus, about one hour after leaving school.

George had started a job at the cheese factory in Bruce Crossing and worked the afternoon shift, so Mother and I had to do the evening milking and chores. No farming had been done at this place for many years, and the fences were virtually nonexistent. The cows were free to roam wherever they could find grass.

With Mother's bad back, it quickly became apparent that I was designated as the cowherder. It's amazing how far a herd of cows can travel between morning and evening milking.

For this first fall year, we kept the cattle inside at night, until pastures could be defined and fences restored. Since the farm was started with nothing, we didn't have a tractor. George was able to find a doodlebug as a substitute. It was the front end of a 1934 Ford, flat head V-8, with everything removed from the firewall rearward. A four-speed International truck transmission and rear axle with single wheels was placed behind the Ford transmission. The driver's seat was set on the floorboard, and the passenger seat was on the gas tank, also on the floorboard. Of course, there was no windshield or roof. The placement of the rear axle provided a short wheelbase.

My first experience driving this thing was typical of my experiences on George's farm. I had been driving our car, with its three-speed transmission, since I was nine years old, and I had also driven tractors from the time I was eight. But the doodlebug was different. A couple of days earlier, George and Uncle Vic had gone fishing using the doodlebug and had buried it in mud. The two men and I went to bring it back. We drove four miles to get as close as possible, bringing shovels, jacks, chains, and a come-along with us.

We walked for a couple of miles through the swamps and low land, along a trail that followed the Middle Branch of the Ontonagon River. The bugs were ferocious. Mosquitos and black flies were so thick, it was almost impossible to avoid inhaling them. We proceeded to lift the doodlebug by placing logs and brush under the wheels, to free the frame from the mud. The men used the come-along to assist in winching it out, as Uncle Vic and I pushed. With the engine running, George and Uncle Vic walked away. George hollered back, "Drive it back to the farm."

As I realized what this meant, I inhaled a mouthful of mosquitos.

I was overcome with panic and fear when I jumped onto the doodlebug. In front of me I saw two shifting levers, one from a Ford car and another one attached and rearward, an extra transmission. It took me a minute to analyze what to do.

I pushed in the clutch and then placed the car transmission in first gear. When I slowly released the clutch, nothing happened. George had left the other transmission in neutral. I had never driven a truck, so where the gears were located in a truck transmission was a guess. I took a chance, shifted and slowly let out the clutch. The engine died. I felt another surge of panic.

It took me at least three attempts before I finally got the engine running, while imagining the six-mile walk home. I tried another gear. The doodlebug moved, but very slowly. Being so scared, I continued driving very slowly, while the engine RPM was high.

Upon arrival at the farm, I was told how stupid I was and that I probably ruined the doodlebug engine. Just what I expected.

Later, I learned where the gear positions were located, but not from George. When the two transmissions were combined, you could actually shift twelve times in forward, and if both were in reverse, you would move forward. Later I had fun driving this doodlebug, but my initiation was only one symptom of the way George treated me.

In this part of the country, cows were only put out to pasture for the night in May, June, July and August. As a result, the cows remain in the barn most of the year. A barn's cleanliness is essential, particularly whenever milk is present, so it was necessary to haul out the manure in the morning and evening before milking. Grain had to be fed to each animal in its stall before milking, and hay was fed to each cow after the milk was removed from the barn.

In order to keep the animals in shape, we occasionally let them out of the barn during the afternoon, the warmest part of the day. They wouldn't go very far and often were willing to come back into the warm barn. However, if they decided they wouldn't go back into the barn, it was necessary to open the front and back doors and chase them around and around the barn until, they—or I—got tired. Of course, this gave me opportunities for a real physical workout.

A barn full of cattle becomes very warm, due to the heat they generate. No additional heat is needed, even in the Upper Peninsula's worst winters.

Per directions from George, I was expected to take one to two weeks off from school in the spring, to fork the manure into a spreader and spread it over the fields. George monitored my output in the fields on a daily basis, to make certain that I wasn't sleeping on the job. This was a normal reaction and constant statement from him. He called me "Sleep Winton."

I was also expected to take time off from school in the fall to dig potatoes and chop and pile wood for the winter. Each fall we would cut at least twenty-five cords of wood (a cord of wood is four feet by four feet by eight feet) for heating the house and cooking in the kitchen.

The best way to breed milking cows for maximum milk is around August, but the gestation period gradually increases as the cow ages. Our herd was in a later time cycle, so breeding took place in late winter and calving in the fall. It is necessary to "dry" the cows for a few weeks in the fall before calving. This is a period when the cow doesn't produce milk, in preparation for the birth of the calf. I write these facts, as it helps to understand the following story.

My half-brother, Joe, was born on October 16, 1952. Two days after my mother and Joe were brought home from the hospital, my mother was rushed back to the Ironwood Hospital to have her gall bladder removed. She was now fifty miles away from home.

That same night, George had one of his recurring stomach attacks. He was in terrible pain, head between his knees, and couldn't straighten up. I took the car and rushed to the neighbors, to ask them to drive to town and call for an ambulance.

The ambulance arrived, and George was loaded and transported to the Veterans Administration Hospital in Iron Mountain, about seventy miles in the opposite direction from Mother. I, at thirteen, and my sister at ten, were home alone with a two-week-old brother and a herd of cattle.

Luckily, Trish knew how to prepare milk for Joe, and we figured out how to change diapers. We put him into his crib for the night and prayed we could find help tomorrow.

After a fitful night with little sleep and a lot of worry, I took care of the morning chores and drove to my Aunt's Lydia's house, to ask if she would come to help care for Joe.

"NO," she said. She had to take care of their cows and family. The next option was to call Aunt Esther in Ontonagon. I drove to town to make the phone call. A lady in town had the only phone exchange in the Trout Creek area, so I had to go to her house. She used the phone exchange board to make the connection. I called Aunt Esther, and she agreed to come immediately.

With Aunt Esther taking care of Joe, Trish went to school as usual. I stayed home from school and cared for the farm, milking morning and night, cooling the milk, and ensuring the milk was picked up by the creamery. We normally milked ten cows by hand, but fortunately three were dry and ready to have their calves. No pens had been prepared for the arrival of these calves, so this was my next project.

During the next few weeks, three calves were born, and I delivered all of them. The calving went without any difficulties, and I remember giving thanks to the Lord. I also started the milking process on the "fresh" cows, a term to describe the new milk coming for the calf. I thought I did a great job.

Mother came home near the end of October. Aunt Esther stayed until she was confident Mother and Trish were able to handle Joe's care. Uncle Art came and took her home.

In the second week of November, a very big snowstorm started raging about noon. By the time evening milking was started, we had at least a foot and a half of new snow. It was coming down in inches per hour.

I was in the process of milking when I saw very dim car headlights approaching. My instinct told me George was coming home, and I was right. He immediately came into the barn, grunted a hello, and proceeded to check the neck chains on each of the cattle. I had let the cows out for exercise just before the snow started and had difficulty getting the bull back into the barn. When I finally got Little Spike into the barn, he had continued to be difficult, so I chained him one link tighter, as he had the habit of working himself loose and I couldn't afford to have this happen again.

George found the chain tighter than usual, and he screamed, "Are you trying to strangle Spike?" He approached me as I was sitting on a stool milking a cow, and he proceeded to kick me a couple of times, knocking me, the milk stool, pail, and milk into the manure gutter. Completely covered in manure and urine, I stormed out of the barn. This was the thanks I got for running the farm while he was in the hospital for four weeks.

I had to undress on the porch and take a shower. Mother asked what happened after she got me some clean clothes. I told her, "George can finish the chores. I'm done. This was his thank-you for the job I did."

George completed the barn chores that night. When he finally came into the house, we got into another screaming match. The problems between us were now completely out in the open. From this point on, our relationship went from bad to worse.

The next couple of years were filled with tension, fear, and down-right anger. So many episodes were experienced that they are too numerous to mention. I was expected to do what I considered an unreasonable amount of labor, while he constantly criticized my weight.

I certainly wasn't a skinny kid like he wanted me to be. I think I was about one hundred thirty pounds when I was thirteen, so I decided to stop eating and went for many days without food. Mother became very worried and tried to make me eat. I refused. I wouldn't even go to the table. When I finally did start to eat again, I mainly ate soda crackers.

My weight went down to about one hundred pounds. The neighbors and relatives started asking if I was sick, and I would deny it. Around this time, tuberculosis was common. I was tested and had an initial positive response to the test. This was a very scary time for me. I didn't feel good anyway, and to have this on my mind was even worse.

As I recall, I had to wait a period of time for a retest. When the retest was finally done, the results were negative, but I was scolded by the doctor and told to gain some weight. What helped me was the end of winter and the start of spring.

Dangerous Work

Yellow and white poplar trees were abundant in our area. In the spring of the year, as the sap rose up the trees, it was customary to harvest this wood, to be used in making paper. This process was called "pulping."

After the trees were felled, their limbs were removed, eight-foot lengths marked, and the bark of the tree trunk was peeled from the trunk. Every fall, the tree trunks would be cut and piled up for removal from the woods in the winter, after the ground had frozen.

In the spring of 1953, when I had just turned fourteen, I took a job to peel pulp for a neighbor. I removed the limbs with an axe, measured and marked eight-foot lengths, and peeled the bark from the downed poplar trees. I was paid five cents per eight-foot length, called a "stick." I also had to trim off the top of the tree where the diameter was not less than four inches in diameter. I was only able to do fifty to sixty sticks per day, while other men and older boys were able to reach eighty per day.

One day, we were on a high bank of the Middle Branch of the Ontonagon River. The bank was extremely steep, and most of the trees were dropped so their tops faced downhill from the stump. It was difficult to stand, as the bank was so steep. I was trying different techniques to better my output, so I would earn more money. I started on a large poplar tree with a diameter at the stump of at least one-and- one-half feet.

I marked the first few sticks, peeled the trunk, removed limbs, and worked my way down the tree. As I neared the top of the tree, I decided to cut it off, and went back to peeling the last sticks. When peeling poplar trees in the spring, there is a lot of liquid between the trunk and bark, and it is very slippery. Without warning, this entire tree trunk suddenly took off down the hill toward the water below. A limb that had not been trimmed tight to the trunk caught my pant leg, and I was being dragged down the hill. My body hit a couple of trees, but the tree pulling me down was miraculously stopped when the tip of the trunk hit a tree. I was banged up quite badly, but alive.

That wasn't my only brush with danger.

In October of 1953, I had to stay home from school for one week to pick potatoes. We had a fairly large potato patch in a sandy half-acre area on the hill behind the house. I had to dig up the potatoes manually, then let them lay uncovered on the ground to dry. Later, I would pick them up and place them in a small two-wheeled wagon that was pulled behind our tractor, which we shared with my stepfather's brother. It was a Farmall B model with a tricycle front end, designed to be used for cultivating. The driver sat on the side between the transmission and the right rear wheel, so he could have a full view of the area beneath him.

I had just finished milking our cows, cooling the milk, and getting it on the milk truck. Then I watched the school bus turn around in our yard after picking up my sister. I remember being very angry. Besides missing school, I had to dig these potatoes by hand when there were machines that could be wheeled over the rows, automatically digging up the potatoes, and the potatoes only had to be picked up! Hand digging was very difficult, and I knew that George would later be checking my work with a fork, to verify that I had dug up all of them. Heaven help me if he found any.

The tractor was parked next to the barn, and because of potential freezing temperatures, the radiator was drained each night, as we couldn't afford antifreeze. I had to fill the radiator with water before starting the tractor. After doing that, I started the tractor, set the rpm above idle, and let it warm up. The throttle on the tractor is a hand-operated vertical lever on the left side of the driver's seat, next to the transmission gear shift lever. It has serrations to hold it in a specific location.

I know I was angry and upset as I jumped onto the tractor to drive it over to the wagon and then to the potato field. Another hard day digging potatoes.

The transmission was designed so that second and fourth gears are in the forward position and very close together. It was easy to mistake what gear you were in, as I was reminded when I accidentally placed the transmission in fourth gear and, with the engine still running fast, I let out the clutch.

The tractor jumped forward, throwing me backward and off balance. I couldn't reach the throttle or clutch. I turned the wheel hard to the right, to avoid running into a tree, and was trying to turn through a gate opening located off the end of the barn. As the tractor made the turn, the left wheel weight, projecting outside the rear tire, hit the gate post, and the tractor was thrown to the right. The momentum of my body carried me to the left. I dropped forward, in front of the left rear wheel. My feet were jammed and caught on the transmission shift lever and fender.

Suddenly I was upside down, hanging onto the steering wheel with my left hand. The lugs of the left tractor tire were tearing at my clothes, and my right hand and body were being dragged under the turning left wheel. I knew I couldn't hold on any longer, and I knew I was going to be dragged, head first, under the rotating tire. My end was here.

Suddenly the front tricycle wheels of the tractor dropped into the hole I had created with the rear wheel of the tractor when "cross hauling" hay into the barn. Miraculously, the tractor engine stalled just as I let go of the steering wheel and my head hit the ground just ahead of the tire.

I was upside down, but alive!

I had a terrible time freeing my feet so I could get out of this position. No one was around to see my position or help as I tried to pull myself together. I will admit that I gave thanks to God for sparing my life.

A number of times, my stepfather had ordered me to fill in this hole. I'm still thankful I didn't do it, and in fact, I never filled it in as long as I lived on the farm. Later, whenever I saw that hole, I gave thanks.

A third near-disaster occurred during the summers of 1953 and 1954, when I was fourteen and fifteen. This occurred when I was preparing hay for the cows' winter feed. This process started by cutting the tall grass of the hay fields, letting it lay and dry, then raking it into rows, piling it into stacks, and using pitch forks to lift the stacks onto a hay wagon before taking it to the barn.

Upon arriving at the barn, a large heavy steel U-shaped hay fork was pushed by hand and body into the hay on the wagon. A voice signal was sounded for the cross hauler at the other end of the barn to drive the tractor away from the barn, pulling a large rope attached to the U-shaped fork. A large load of hay from the hay wagon was lifted. When the U-shaped fork reached the top of the barn, it was latched into the "carriage," located on a track above the hay wagon, and rolled into the barn. When the hay reached the desired spot in the barn, the person inside the hay loft would yell and the loader would release the hay from the fork.

The cross hauler would then back the tractor to the barn, and the loader would manually pull the "carriage," with U fork, outside the barn and let it drop to the hay wagon for the next bunch of hay to be lifted. Depending on the size of wagon and the height of the hay stack on the wagon, it could take between four and six times to unload the entire load in the wagon.

On one occasion, when I was fifteen, I was up in the hayloft directing where the hay was to be dropped. I had directed a drop, and the "carriage" continued to roll to the back of the barn. I had started to spread out the hay as the U fork and "carriage" were being pulled back to the wagon. I heard a scream and the whine of a rope going through a pulley. I didn't have time to move. The U fork brushed the side of my head, slid down my leg, and stuck in the hay. A near hit.

The final event of my tenure on the farm occurred at the end of August 1954. George wanted only a few swaths of hay cut each day. That way, if it rained, we would only lose a small amount. We did lose a day's worth of hay due to rain, but the process was taking forever. The next day, I listened to the weather forecast. Based on the forecast and my personal belief that it wouldn't rain for a few days, I dumped (cut down) all the remaining hay on the field.

That took me almost all day. When George came home from working at the local creamery, he was livid. The hay was so thick that it took two days to dry. I worked feverishly to turn over the cut hay to assist with its drying. I was successful. It was ready to be piled and made ready to be loaded on a wagon and brought to the barn.

I got my mother and sister to help pile the hay, and I worked until the dew started to form. The next day, George took off from work, hired a neighbor, and we started to bring the hay to the barn. It took all day, but we did it. I got the cows from the pasture and into the barn late, maybe seven o'clock, but the U.P. remained light until about ten o'clock at that time of year.

After I finished milking, George told me to bring in the left-over hay that had been thrown off the wagon when the hay loads were unloaded. I was exhausted and merely said, "I'll do it to-morrow." I turned away and was leaving the barn when my step-father picked up a pitchfork and stabbed it into my back.

As George pulled the pitchfork out, I reached down and grabbed a two-by-four chunk of wood. As I turned around, I swung it at his head. It just missed his face, but it knocked his hat off. He turned and ran, with me after him, yelling, "I'll kill you!" We ran until I stopped. A pitchfork prong into the body usually doesn't bleed very much, as a vacuum is created when it's removed. But it hurts like hell, and the wound can easily become infected. Since that day, over the years, I've had severe muscle issues in those areas.

I slammed into the house and told my mother, "Either he or I will have to leave or one of us will be dead by spring—and it won't be me." She cried, but finally said I should go.

Thus ended my life at home. Within three weeks, I had moved to Ontonagon. I didn't return to the farm for four years.

CHAPTER FIVE

Leaving Home

I LEFT THE FARM in Trout Creek the second week of school during my sophomore year, the fall of 1954. I had previously made tentative arrangements to live with my half-brother and his wife, Lloyd and Hazel Winton, and their son and daughter in Iron River. Lloyd had told me many times that I could come and live with them when it got too difficult on the farm. I felt this was my first option, and a good one. But when I actually called to ask about making the move, I was quickly turned away.

Next, I called my mother's sister, Aunt Esther, who lived in Ontonagon, to see if I could live with them. We agreed that I would room and board with them for my remaining three years of high school, if I paid them thirty dollars per month. I was now receiving a monthly thirty-five-dollar Social Security benefit as a result of my father's death in 1946. My aunt agreed that for the money, she would do my laundry and provide meals—if I was there when she served dinner. I was to sleep on a fold-away day bed in the living room, which would need to be folded and stored each morning. Of course, she added, I had to behave myself or I would be put out. And, if I left for any period of time, I didn't have to pay the monthly fee.

Wow! I only had five dollars to take care of buying clothes, Brylcream for my DA hair style (Elvis style), soap and cream for my acne, haircuts (another reason for the DA hair style), school supplies, entertainment, etc. It was obvious to me that finding a job was the order of the day—and hopefully a job that would pay well.

Aunt Esther and Uncle Art drove to Trout Creek the next day to get me. I had the most difficult feelings leaving my sister, Trish, knowing she would be all alone in that household. We did a lot of crying. I tried to reassure her that I wasn't going far and we would often see each other. Mother also was crying, but she gave me a hug and whispered, "God is with you."

I registered at the school in Ontonagon the same day I left the farm. Ontonagon schools had been in session for two weeks, so I wanted to catch up and keep up with all my classes.

Two weeks later, I was taken from class to Mr. Webber's office. The high school principal and Mr. Keefer, the Ontonagon Schools superintendent, were waiting for me. They informed me that I might have to pay high school tuition since I wasn't living with my parents, nor did I have a legal guardian. I told them, "I'm on my own. I can't pay tuition, and I will NOT go back to Trout Creek, PERIOD."

Mr. Keefer asked, "But what will you do?"

I spoke firmly. "I'll leave and find a place somewhere, maybe between here and Texas."

"But you are under age. You can't do that," they responded.

I almost considered this a challenge, but had sense enough to keep my mouth shut. They seemed to be concerned and asked me not to do anything at this time, as they wanted to see if they might have other options. They told me to return to my class and not to worry.

A month later, I was again directed to Mr. Webber's office and found Mr. Keefer there again. With what I detected to be faint smiles, they informed me that since I was in the same county as Trout Creek, they were able to divert the state funds from Trout Creek to Ontonagon. This had been accomplished, and I shouldn't worry about this situation anymore. However, they added that I couldn't participate in school athletic activities until the second semester of the school year.

Wow, God was certainly looking after me, as this tuition episode wouldn't have been possible if I had gone to my brother's house in Iron River.

I had always received high grades throughout my schooling in Trout Creek, and I quickly demonstrated I could get top grades in Ontonagon. Very early in my new sophomore year, I was asked if I would accept running for Student Council Representative for the sophomore class, and I was elected.

1936 Chevy Coupe with rumble seat and Pat

Tricia

Back: Bruno H., Victor Aho, Lydia, Sandy, Marylou, Esther
Front: Marvin, Pat, Tricia, Joan

Pat and Tricia 1945 or '46
Ontonagon

Pat's mother during Easter, 1936

Mother at 12 YOA and Grandma

105 S. 70th Street, Houston, Texas

My mother's parents, Kreeta and Antti Hietala, immigrated
from Finland at the turn of the last century, met in
Michigan, and homesteaded a farm.

Pat with his NEW Schwinn bike

Mother in about 1952
(Note the milk cans)

1952 family farm house

The little house built in 1947

Bulldozing a logging road

Wilbur Winton Dies Suddenly; Rites Tomorrow

Wilbur J. Winton, 47, former Bates township resident, died suddenly Sunday evening at his home in Ontonagon.

He was stricken suddenly at 5:30 p. m. while seated at the supper table with his family. He had finished his meal and was reaching for a cigarette when he fell dead. The seizure came without warning, although Winton had been aware of a heart condition for the last four years.

Funeral services will be held at the funeral chapel in Ontonagon Wednesday at 2 p. m. and interment will be made in the Ontonagon cemetery. A number of west side friends will attend the rites.

Winton was born in Bates township August 9, 1899, attended Bates schools and the Iron River high school, and was employed by the Drott Tractor company for a number of years as a salesman. For many years he had been a tractor and dragline operator and tractor maintenance man.

He left here about 1941 for Houston, Texas where he resided for three years. He had lived in Ontonagon for three years.

Surviving are his wife, Irene, formerly of Trout Creek, and two children, Patrick and Patricia; four sons by a previous marriage, Lester, Earl and Lloyd of Iron River, and Henry of Oshkosh; two brothers, Ralph Winton, manager of the Iron River state liquor store, and Walter Winton, and one sister, Mrs. Fred Comish, of Bates township.

For several years Mr. Winton had been a traveling representative and foreman for Earl Johnson and Rudy Passamoni, excavating contractors.

Dad's obituary

Dad's Drott tractor sales

I told them, 'I'm on my own.
I can't pay tuition, and I will NOT
go back to Trout Creek, PERIOD.'

CHAPTER SIX

My First Job

AFTER CONSIDERABLE investigations into stores, restaurants, and gas stations, it became apparent that no-one would hire a fifteen-year-old boy. I was told that parental approval and special work papers were required, and I had no one to sign those papers. Still, I continued to ask kids in school if they had any ideas or knew of someone who would hire me. Finally, a fellow in my math class told me he was going to give up his paper route. His parents had upped his allowance, and delivering papers in the snow and cold wasn't fun.

The *Ironwood Daily Globe* representative originally took the position that I may not be reliable. I asked my Aunt Esther to talk to the representative, and after a phone call from her and meetings with me, I was given the job.

The paper route was in the area where I lived, so I wouldn't have to walk excessive distances to deliver papers. The route had about twenty-five subscribers, and the homes were quite close together. The daily ritual, Monday through Friday during the school year, was to walk to town from school, pick up the papers, and walk the route I had carefully laid out.

Some subscribers were happy, and some complained, but after some time, all seemed to be satisfied. On Saturdays I walked from my aunt's house to town to pick up the papers. The paper cost fifty cents per week, and I received five cents per subscriber per week. This one dollar and twenty-five cents per week might allow me to see a movie, and it might even give me an opportunity to ask a girl to go with me. But I wondered if any fathers would allow their daughters to go out with a boy who had no parents and boarded with relatives.

I never enjoyed collecting on the required Thursday nights. Most people were not home, so the collection often continued through Saturday, when I was required to pay the representative. Once in a while, I even received a tip.

I continued to deliver newspapers until my sophomore school year ended. That was when I joined the carnival.

It became apparent that no one would hire a fifteen-year-old boy without parents or guardians.

CHAPTER SEVEN

The Winter Coat

WHEN I ARRIVED IN ONTONAGON in the second week of September, 1954, school had already started, and my wardrobe was very limited: a single pair of shoes, a couple pairs of blue jeans, several shirts, and a light jacket. The jacket certainly wouldn't be sufficient for the winter season.

In this part of the country, winter is long and cold. The snow usually arrives by mid-November, and I remember finding snow in the woods at the end of May. Snow accumulation in the Upper Peninsula through the winter is measured in hundreds of inches. Winter temperatures during these years ranged between twenty degrees Fahrenheit and minus-twenty degrees, with periods of a week or two at minus-thirty degrees. In contrast, we would experience a week or two in the summer at more than one hundred degrees.

That November, the weather turned very cold, forcing me to go shopping for a winter coat. I went to the only clothing store in town, Mazurek's, and started looking at jackets. Of course, I was totally focused only on the price tags. Mr. Mazurek walked up to me and asked, "Can I help you?"

I told him that I needed a winter coat, but I was only able to pay five dollars per month. I now had five dollars cash with me. He wanted to know more about me and where I lived. I told him I was from Trout Creek, now rooming and boarding at Esther and

Art Bessen's house, and that I was a sophomore at Ontonagon High School. He told me that the Bessens had been very good customers. "I know Art quite well." He stepped away as I continued to look at the price tags.

When he returned, he told me, "Since you have five dollars now, I will limit your purchase to twenty dollars. Be certain you pay on the first of the month."

I found a red, single-layered wool jacket with buttons down the front for sixteen dollars. It wasn't going to be really warm, but it was better than what I had. I paid Mr. Mazurek six dollars, as I had a dollar in change, and left with the coat. I paid five dollars for the next two months, always on the first of the month. I wore that coat all through high school, even in the minus-twenty and minus-thirty-degree weather. I guess that might be why I can't wear a bulky coat today.

Mr. Mazurek was another example of someone giving me a break, and of me living up to my commitment.

Snow accumulation in the Upper Peninsula through the winter is measured in hundreds of inches.

CHAPTER EIGHT

A Carnival Life for Me

AFTER SCHOOL let out at the end of May in 1955, I was on a quest to find a job that would supplement my income. Up to this time, my only sources of support were from the paper route and the five dollars per month left over after paying my aunt from the monthly Social Security check. In total, this wasn't going to provide sufficient income to purchase clothes and other necessities for the coming junior year.

Early in June, the Skerbeck Carnival came to town. With a home base in Venice, Florida, the Skerbeck Carnival had been coming to the Upper Peninsula of Michigan for many years. Their size was geared to small communities and areas, like Ontonagon. As I recall, it remained in town for three or four nights. When I ran across it, the tents had already been set up on the Rockland Road, just south of the railroad tracks, on the Stricklands' property.

Max Alexander and I were at the pool hall talking about what we were going to do for the summer. The mutual discussion centered on how we might earn some money. "I've scoped out the carnival and inquired about joining before they move to the next location," Max told me. "They're looking for men to join them, as this is their normal first stop when they come to the U.P."

My immediate response was, "Wow, what a great idea! We can earn money and experience a huge adventure at the same time!"

We decided to go to the carnival and make more specific inquiries. As we rode there in Max's car, Max said, "I'm ready to go, but I won't go unless you also go."

"I'm ready," I said. "I'll go if the job is okay. By the way, I can do whatever I want."

We found the carnival owner and asked Mr. Skerbeck about jobs.

"Are you eighteen? Can you drive a semi-tractor and trailer?" he asked us.

Our response was in unison. "Of course we're eighteen." (I was sixteen, and Max was seventeen.) Then I said, "I have extensive experience driving semi's and heavy equipment." Max quickly added, "My father owns a local trucking business, and I've driven semi's."

I told Mr. Skerbeck that I had grown up on a farm driving trucks—"and I can back two- or four-wheel trailers with precision and accuracy."

His next question: "Can you be here, ready to go to work in two days and be prepared to work all night?"

I looked at Max. We both shrugged our shoulders and said, "Yes, of course. What time should we be here?"

We were introduced to the manager of operations under Mr. Skerbeck, who told us we were guaranteed three meals a day, a bunk in a semi-trailer specially fitted for sleeping, and we would be paid ten dollars per day. To our relief, he said, "You're both hired. Give me your Social Security numbers, and be here two nights from now at ten o'clock sharp." He also told us that he'd assign each of us to a man in charge of one of the carnival rides. "You'll do whatever he wants, and you'll work all night to tear his ride down, pack it in the trucks, and be ready to depart at dawn. Understood?"

Understood.

I told my aunt that I had a job with the carnival, but I don't recall any reaction. It wouldn't have made any difference, as she knew I was always looking for a way to earn money.

Wow! We were about to go traveling, earning money, and, based on what I observed in Ontonagon, we could expect a lot of girls following the carnival guys. I was on cloud nine.

As soon as I arrived for my new job, I was assigned to Chief, a First Nation Indian, who was in charge of the merry-go-round. He was well over six feet tall and all muscle. Others advised me not to argue with him—"as he has a real bad temper." I heard Chief was also known for hurting guys he didn't like.

About eleven o'clock that night, Max and I and the other men started to tear down the carnival. We had the merry-go-round on the trucks by four o'clock in the morning. I was then told to go and assist with the tilt-a-whirl, where Max was assigned. Art was the guy in charge of the tilt-a-whirl, and he was a filthy-mouthed, mean man—and the dirtiest guy on the outside I had ever encountered. Every other word was a curse word, and he only knew how to scream orders.

We finished in time for a quick breakfast and were ordered to our trucks, to begin our trip to Lake Linden. I was assigned a long bed stake truck with at least a twenty-four-foot trailer. Max had a semi tractor and trailer.

The route to Lake Linden required us to drive down a very steep two-mile grade, then directly onto the old bridge crossing the Keweenaw Waterway that led into the city of Hancock.

A sharp turn to the left was right at the bottom of the grade. I had been on this bridge in a car, and I knew it was very narrow with only two lanes. I overheard experienced carnival guys question what would happen if two semi-trucks met on the bridge. My fears were building.

We were all ordered to stop at the top of the hill, down shift, and then maintain distance with NO passing. I was second in line, following a semi driven by the manager of operations. At the top of the grade, he pulled over, stopped, and waved at me to stop next to him. "Go ahead, first in line cross the bridge, and pull over when I'm clear on the other side," he said.

I recall the fear I felt at that moment, and praying was the only thing I could do. Fortunately, going down the grade went okay, and I made the sharp left turn without any tires touching the center lane markings.

Oh my gosh, that bridge was so narrow. When I looked forward, I saw two semi's coming toward me. I was going very slowly, and so were they. I said my prayers while looking at the right side of the bridge and its outer railing. I knew what my overhang load distance was, and I kept trying to gauge where the semi-trailers would be in relation to me.

The first went by, no metal crunching. Now for the second. At last, I was clear. "Thank you, Lord!" On the other side and clear of the bridge, I pulled over to wait. The manager of operations immediately pulled next to me, gave me the high sign, and waved for me to follow him.

That day, after setting up the rides, we were called to a group meeting. Mr. Skerbeck called me up to the front and told the group that I was one of the best drivers of the day, and said they all should drive like me. I was so embarrassed, and immediately began to worry if I was going to have issues with the other guys now.

The semi-truck trailer held fifteen narrow sleeping bunks, three high, and arranged around the interior of the trailer. The door was at the trailer's front right side. Upon entering, I saw a small closet for hanging clothes. Adjacent to the closet was a wash basin on a stand for washing hands and faces. A shaving mirror hung on the wall above the wash basin. Water for the basin had to brought in from outside. I was thankful to be assigned to a lower bunk near the door. All these years later, I remember how bad that trailer smelled at times. Some of these guys certainly didn't take a bath very often, even though a separate trailer with clean showers and toilets was always situated near the sleeping trailer.

My assignment to the merry-go-round was easy. Chief showed me how to run the ride. Generally, my job was to collect tickets and watch for the safety of the riders. Communication between Chief and me was minimal, except for "You collect the tickets" or "I am going to take a piss, so you watch over the ride." One evening at our first stop, I had just removed my bright red corduroy shirt from the common closet and put it on when Chief stepped forward and ordered, "Give me that shirt. I'm wearing it tonight."

I stepped back and said, "This is my shirt. If you want it, you'll have to take it off me."

The guys still in the trailer and those who had just exited heard these words, hollered "Fight!" and began to crowd around. Chief was evidently surprised at my defiance and threatened to beat me to a pulp. I had heard stories about his abilities to fight. Someone told me that once he started, he didn't back off. I said again, "You'll have to take it off me. I'm not afraid of you."

Suddenly, Chief reached into the closet and pulled out a mint green jacket with a horizontal Indian design in a band around the chest. He said, "You wear this, and I'll wear your shirt."

"Okay," I responded, feeling surprised and relieved. I exchanged shirt for jacket. Upon exiting the trailer, one of the guys told me that no one ever touched Chief's jacket, and he had badly beaten a guy who tried it on. From that time onwards, Chief and I were buddies.

Often after the show was closed, Chief would buy a six pack of beer and we would drink and talk. He told me of his upbringing and his negative feelings about life. His mother had him out of wedlock, and she had many boyfriends. When he was seven, his mother and boyfriend had broken out a window in a gas station and forced him inside to steal whatever was available. He suspected his mother had called the police, as they arrived when he was in the station. He was arrested and placed in an all-white orphanage, where he learned how to fight real fast.

At one of the carnival stops, we were informed the trucks and trailers needed to be cleaned. I was washing my truck and trailer when I heard a loud commotion, and I ran to see what was happening.

Max had decided to move his tractor and trailer to make it easier to wash. His trailer was used to haul the tilt-a-whirl's large, heavy, center-drive unit. At setup in a new location, the trailer was backed up to the precise location where the tilt-a-whirl would be assembled. The center piece was winched-down on steel tracks to its location. The trailer was then carefully moved away, keeping it in a straight line so it could be returned and the center-drive winched back onto the trailer. Max's action had removed this carefully maintained location, and now the trailer would be extremely difficult, if not impossible, to get back into alignment.

"Max, what in the world were you thinking?" was my reaction as I ran toward him. Art was screaming at Max for moving the trailer, and a fight had already started. Max didn't have a chance.

He was getting beaten up really bad. I moved forward in the crowd, ready to step in to help Max. As Max got up from the ground, he had a steel tent stake in his hand, ready to swing it at Art. I'm screaming, "Max, hit him." He didn't. Art moved in for the finish. When Max was down and out, Art turned on me. The first couple of swings missed. I did get one solid punch. I caught a punch on the side of my head and went down. As I started to get up, I was pushed down. Upon looking up, I saw Chief standing over me, hitting Art.

The fight was over in seconds, and Chief reached down to pull me up. He turned to the group and said, "No one is ever to touch Pat again. If you do, you will deal with me."

From that time on, I didn't worry about being bothered or threatened.

Max and I had been gone for about two and half weeks when I was called to Mr. Skerbeck's trailer and given a special-delivery letter that had been forwarded a couple of times. It was from my mother. How did she find me? I opened the letter. It was short and to the point. She had finally heard I had left with the carnival, and she was angry. She wrote to tell me that if I wasn't back in Ontonagon by a specific date—now only two days away—she would call the State Police to come and get me.

First, I went in search of Chief and told him some of the details. I also asked him to keep the news to himself. He said he would. I felt bad leaving him, as he was a friend I wish I could have gotten to know better and helped him, if only by listening.

I found Mr. Skerbeck, and without explanation said, "My mother needs me."

"I'm sorry to lose you," he told me, saying I was an excellent worker. "If you ever want a job again, come and see me."

I collected my gross pay, paid the cook, and with one hundred dollars in my pocket, packed my things. When I informed Max of the change in plans, he decided to join me. We hitch-hiked the fifty miles back to Ontonagon.

Now I had to decide what to do for the rest of the summer.

Two years later, in the summer of 1957, the Skerbeck Carnival was back in the U.P., and I inquired about Chief. I was told that he was in prison. I wasn't necessarily surprised, but I was sorry.

CHAPTER NINE

Life as a Farm Hand

THE SUMMER between my sophomore and junior years was fast moving. I had already worked three weeks with the Skerbeck Carnival, saving June's Social Security payment plus netting about one hundred dollars from the carnival. Now I needed to find other employment.

I was constantly calculating my finances. If I could earn room and board for the next two months, I would be able to save the thirty dollars per month from Social Security, rather than pay it to my aunt. Income, in addition to room and board, would be fantastic.

As I mentioned earlier, my grandparents had individually immigrated from Finland and met in the Copper Country. After they married in 1901, they homesteaded on eighty acres in Interior Township, near Trout Creek. My Aunt Lydia and her husband, Bruno Helsius, had moved onto the grandparents' original homestead after World War II. They were milking twelve to fifteen cows, and my cousin Marvin had to do most of the work, since Bruno worked at the Trout Creek sawmill.

Before I joined the carnival, they asked if I wanted to come and help them during haying season. They couldn't pay me, but they offered free room and board. I contacted Aunt Lydia and asked if the offer to work was still possible. She told me to come right away. I thanked her and promised I'd leave immediately.

I looked forward to working with my cousin and best friend, Marvin. Marvin and I were born the same year, but when his family moved to Trout Creek from Ohio, he was held back one school year. I never understood this, as he was very smart and had very high grades in school.

We had lived next door to each other for four years after my father died. We fished, hunted, and trapped together, and we were in the same confirmation class in our church. We bought Boy Scout handbooks, and even though there wasn't a Boy Scout troop in the area, we earned badges on our own.

I hitchhiked the more than thirty miles to the Helsius's farm. They were happy to see me, as they were ready to begin haying.

The work day consisted of getting up, fetching cows, cleaning the barn, milking, cooling the milk, and returning the cows to pasture. We took a short break for a normal breakfast of coffee, eggs, and potatoes. The alfalfa field was ready, so we began cutting it as soon as I arrived. When the hay was dry, we raked it into windrows, piled it, loaded the wagon, and took it to the barn. I set the fork into the loose hay on the wagon, and when ready, I yelled to Aunt Lydia to start cross-hauling the hay into the barn.

Marvin whistled when he wanted to release the hay from the fork, and he spread the hay in the hay loft. The drop of hay caused slack in the cross-haul rope, so Aunt Lydia would know to return for the next lift. Late each afternoon, we stopped haying to complete the evening milking, ate dinner, and enjoyed free time.

By the second week in July, we had completed haying.
I thanked Aunt Lydia, said goodbye to Marvin, and hitchhiked to Painesville.

Earlier that summer, at the Fourth of July celebration in Bruce Crossing, I was told that Herman Manty, a farmer in Painesville, was looking for a farm hand to help him make hay.

I had previously met Herman, and I went in search of him. When I found him, he remembered me.

Herman was a bachelor with a reputation for taking advantage of people, so I planned to be very specific about the job after asking if he was hiring someone. He wanted to know more about my situation. I assumed he knew of my departure from my abusive stepfather. We talked, and he agreed to hire me. I would eat at his brother's house next door, sleep at Herman's house, and work making hay. If it rained, I would saw into eight-foot lengths the pulp logs that had been peeled in the spring.

My pay, after room and board, would be twenty dollars per week.

I told him I had two more weeks of haying at the Helsius farm, and I would be able to start on Monday of the third week of July. He said, "That's perfect."

Herman was a tough task master and led the pace of the day. He was about sixty years old and was in great physical condition. I was cutting hay by seven o'clock in the morning. He started raking the hay that had been cut the prior day around ten o'clock, after the dew was dried off by the sun. Then right after lunch, he began baling the hay, and I finished raking. I then picked up the bales and slid them onto a special sled he had built. To make the hay sled, he bolted planked hard wood about eight feet wide and twenty feet long together. This way I didn't have to lift the bales. I just had to slide the forty-pound hay bales onto the sled and then stack them and deliver them to the barn.

As soon as Herman completed baling, he drove the tractor, pulling the sled, while I hooked the bales as we passed by, and stacked them. The sled load was brought near the barn and stopped at the conveyor. Herman placed the bales on the conveyor, which carried them upward and into the barn, where I stacked them. All of the bales made that day were in the barn by seven o'clock at night. Time for dinner.

All our meals were prepared at the adjacent farmhouse, which was owned by Herman's brother and family. Mrs. Yalmer

Manty was a wonderful cook. Her meals were outstanding, the best I had eaten since my mother's cooking. And the meal was even better because I was served by a delightful girl, Herman's niece Marylyn. She made certain I had plenty to eat. Marylyn had been in my confirmation class, but I didn't have the opportunity to know her before this. She seemed to be around us all the time, but, under the watchful eye of Herman.

In three weeks, we completed Herman's project, estimated at eighty to one hundred tons of hay, and I wanted to be paid so I could return to Ontonagon. I anticipated problems, so I was mentally prepared when I asked for my sixty dollars.

Herman responded, "I don't have any money." He opened his empty wallet. Well, he has lived up to his reputation, I thought. He continued, "But I'm willing to give you this watch, worth at least one hundred dollars." He opened a drawer and pulled out a wrist watch.

I was ready for this run-around. "I know all about your ways of cheating people, and you're going to pay me the sixty dollars you promised. If you don't pay me now, I'm going to your brother Yalmer and tell him what you're doing." I got right in his face, ready for a fight.

Herman didn't back away, but he brought up the fact that Melvin Manty, Yalmer's twenty-two-year-old son, and I had been going out on Friday and Saturday nights, using Herman's gas from his storage tank. This was true! Melvin told me he did this all the time.

Herman went to his bedroom and returned with a fifty-dollar bill in his hand. "This is all you're going to get," he said, and handed me the bill. I took it, grabbed my bag, walked the mile to M-28, and hitchhiked back to Ontonagon.

Looking back on the Herman experience helped me to understand that sometimes it is best to take what you can and walk, rather than argue.

I was proud of my sixteen-year-old summer, earning room

and board and one hundred dollars from the carnival, as well as fifty dollars from Herman Manty. I had also saved Social Security from June, July, and part of August. I had enough money to buy school clothes and then some.

I continued to look for work during my junior school year.

An opportunity came in the early spring of 1956. My aunt attended church with a Polish couple who had decided to look for help to milk their twenty-five cows, as the husband was having health issues. They had a full-time man working for them, but the chores were too much for him alone. My aunt told them I was interested in working, and they agreed to meet me.

Before going to meet them, I learned that the school bus passed by their farm, so I would have a ride to and from school if I worked there. I walked to their farm and introduced myself. I don't recall their names, so I will only refer to them as husband, wife, and worker. After some discussion, I confirmed they milked twenty-five cows with milking machines, and they needed someone to assist with the morning and evening milking. They offered room and board and a few dollars a week.

This was another opportunity to save the thirty-five dollars from Social Security, so I accepted.

I was awakened at 3:45 each morning, and I prepared the barn for the cows. The worker always brought all the cows from the pasture, as he knew how to handle them. He didn't want my help. I cleaned out the manure if the cows had been in the barn all night.

Prior to milking, about 5:30, we went into the house for breakfast. I have never, before or since, experienced such a breakfast. It started with barley soup, followed by a full meal of meat, potatoes, vegetables, and plenty of freshly baked bread and coffee. A real he-man meal.

After breakfast, we milked the cows with automatic milkers taken to each cow's stall. I was very impressed with the cleanliness demanded by the husband and worker. My first job was to wash the udder. At first, I was closely supervised by the worker. After the milker was removed from the cows' udders, I was assigned to "strip" the remaining milk from the udders. You see, not all the milk is taken from the udder with this type of milking machine, so it's necessary to remove the remaining milk. If this isn't done, or not done properly, mastitis infection of the udder can occur, and the milk can't be consumed. This infection is very difficult to eliminate.

When the milk was cooled and ready for pickup, I cleaned up and was ready for the school bus at eight o'clock.

As soon as I jumped off the afternoon school bus, I changed into my barn clothes and went to the barn to prepare for the evening milking process. Then came dinner.

The normal ritual was to eat the morning leftovers for dinner, milk the cows, and finish about seven o'clock that night, at which time everyone went to bed.

After two or three weeks, this repetitive process was getting very boring. I needed to go to town rather than to bed. I started walking to town and returning between ten and eleven o'clock at night. The couple had to awaken me on a couple of mornings, and our relationship started to change. Nothing was said, but some strange assignments were made.

On weekends, they gave me a bucket and an umbrella, if it was raining, and told me to go out into the oat fields (and they had many acres), to hand-pick rocks and weeds. After a couple of weekends picking rocks and pulling weeds, I told them, "I quit."

They didn't seem upset. I believe they were happy to have me leave. Maybe the husband had recovered from his health issue. In May, I would be seventeen, and I didn't mind the work, but I wasn't a slave.

I remember deciding that I would never again work on a farm unless I owned it. Farm work was hard and required long hours. I was willing to work, but I needed to be treated as a young man. I needed the people who hired me to evaluate and talk to me if I wasn't doing what was expected.

My experience on the farm with my abusive stepfather, summer hay-making, and then this strange farming couple showed me I had little or no future growth opportunities on a farm. I decided I'd better take all the classes I could possibly take in my remaining year of high school. Then I would consider joining the Air Force or finding some way to go to college.

I wanted to lead and advance myself, not stay the same or just follow others.

CHAPTER TEN

My High School Years

IN THE FALL of 1954, I started my sophomore year in Trout Creek. After leaving the family farm, I continued as a sophomore in Ontonagon High School. Going from a class of nine to a class of fifty-five was a dramatic change for me. The Ontonagon High School had also recently gone through a lot of changes, due to the additional high school students being bussed from White Pine, twenty miles west of Ontonagon.

This company mining town was built in 1953, when the White Pine Copper/Silver Mine was reopened. Because there were all those other new students, it was easier for me to fit into this new environment. Also, I had gone to Ontonagon schools for my kindergarten thru second grades, with many of the same students. Even though we didn't remember each other, it had a positive impact on being accepted.

For some unknown reason, I was almost immediately elected to be the Student Council representative from my sophomore class. I found this experience exciting, and I put much effort into this responsibility. I continued to be our representative in our junior year. At the beginning of our senior year, someone recommended I run for Student Council president. Suddenly a number of class-mates supported this effort, and I had a campaign committee.

I was running against an extremely popular, rich, well-known opponent from the junior class. A group of girl classmates created skits that they presented. My opponent and I debated before the entire high school. When the votes were tallied, I was declared the winner. For some reason, a song was written for one of the skits and titled "Honey Bun." I can't remember what this was all about, but it helped me win. I was often kidded about this when we got together at reunions.

As Student Council president, I had the privilege of introducing the forty-first Michigan governor, G. Mennen Williams (Soapy Williams), to the student body.

Ontonagon High School offered many elective classes, in addition to the basic state requirements. This was new to me, and I decided since I was on my own and didn't think I could go to college that I would take all the classes offered that might make up for not going to college.

As an example, I took all math and science classes rather than shop and drafting. I even took typing, since I felt it would help me prepare papers for writing in the future. I was the only guy in the class, and I had a lot of fun with the girls. I even achieved one hundred words per minute. The girls tried to convince me to take shorthand, but I drew the line and refused. I later learned this was a mistake, as it would have been a great asset in many of my future classes and business meetings.

Due to the fact that Trout Creek didn't offer Algebra in the ninth grade, I was behind my classmates and had to take it in Ontonagon with freshmen. I took Geometry in my junior year, and Advanced Algebra the first semester of my senior year.

At the beginning of the second semester as a senior, I was taking Solid Geometry and knew I wasn't going to have the opportunity to take Trigonometry unless I had help. Mrs. Neumann taught all mathematic classes. She was very tough and disciplined. I decided to approach her and ask if she would tutor me in Trigonometry during the study hall hour she led, as it also was my study hall.

She thought about my request for a moment, and responded, "Only in the study hall. I'll give assignments and tests. I'll answer your questions. But if you falter in any way, I'll stop. It's up to you."

I didn't even hesitate to agree, and I was given my first assignment. She answered questions only in study hall and carefully watched over me during tests. I completed Trigonometry and Solid Geometry in the second semester of my senior year with an A minus in both.

CHAPTER ELEVEN

The Pool Hall

THE THREE SCHOOL YEARS I spent living with Aunt Esther and Uncle Art were a real challenge. The rules were established that dinner was at 5:30, and if I was not present, I couldn't count on a dinner to be saved. Unfortunately, with my work and activities, I was seldom there on time. I also didn't enjoy evenings at their home since I slept in the living room on a fold-away bed and therefore had no privacy. They often had company visiting in the living room, so my bed had to be unfolded each night and put away each morning.

I didn't complain, as I certainly appreciated and welcomed having a place to live. I often walked the mile and a half to the local pool hall. There I could talk to friends decide to walk through town or play pool.

The hall had at least four eight-ball tables and a snooker table. Located above the bowling alley, it was managed by a very nice elderly couple who wanted to provide a place for the young people to gather. They maintained a snack bar, and charged ten cents a game for standard eight-ball pool. Since I didn't have any extra money, I quickly learned to play pool and win.

The rule was the loser would pay the ten cents, so I was always looking for someone to beat. Of course, winning wasn't always possible, and many a night was spent sitting on a stool and watching others play.

After the evening at the pool hall, the mile and a half walk home was always refreshing, even if it was raining or snowing. In the winter, the four-to-six-foot snow banks covered the sidewalk, so walking on the blacktop street was necessary. Single street lights hung over the street at certain intervals. The wind would cause them to swing, and strange shadows would be displayed on the street and snow banks.

On clear nights, the moon and stars would fill the sky when I walked between street lights. Suddenly the Northern Lights or Aurora Borealis might light up the sky, and I had to stop and admire God's wonderful creation. My normal arrival at home was eleven o'clock.

Since I didn't have any extra
money, I quickly learned to
play pool and win.

CHAPTER TWELVE

High School Sports

I STRONGLY WANTED to continue playing basketball in Ontonagon, as it was the sport of Trout Creek. During the winter, Mr. Bruce Warren, coach and teacher at Trout Creek, would begin teaching basketball to third graders when they had recess in the gymnasium. The Trout Creek High School basketball team was known throughout Michigan for winning Class E State Championships.

The State of Michigan sport rules dictated that anyone transferring schools had to wait until the next semester in order to join a high school sports team. I was, therefore, ineligible to play basketball or any sport until the second semester.

Football was well underway when I started in Ontonagon in September, as practice had started in mid-August. The coach of the football, basketball, and baseball teams was also a shop teacher. His rule was if you wanted to play basketball, you had to go out for football. During a meeting with him and the junior varsity basketball coach, I was told I could practice with the football team and the junior high basketball team and assist the coaches in both sports until I became eligible to play basketball. If I was good enough, they would decide if I actually would be on the junior varsity basketball team.

I had never played football, and the guys were already in great shape. I was given a practice uniform, and I eagerly joined the practice. What a surprise on the first day. After calisthenics, we had to take a football and run at a defensive team player. My first experience was to run at the biggest, toughest guy on defense. I was in fairly good shape, but as I ran at him, I was running as you would run a race, straight up. As he hit me, he lifted me in the air and dropped me on my back, knocking the wind out of me. I think he was as surprised as I was. That never happened again. John and I became very good friends, and he remembers this incident to this day.

I managed to be at football practice while keeping my newspaper route. It was tough, as I normally didn't return home until late, well after dinner had been served. Aunt Esther was somewhat forgiving, and she would try to keep some of their dinner for me. I don't remember being hungry, but I do know that I often ate standing up and on the run.

Every Thursday's dinner was a bowl of rice topped with fresh or home canned berries. There was always a bowl of cold rice with fruit in the refrigerator. I still can't eat cold rice to this day.

I assisted the referees by handling the ten-yard chains for that football season, during the games at home and away. I practiced with the junior varsity basketball team and also assisted the coach, Mr. Zimmerman, during the games. I finally started my first official junior varsity basketball game late in January and finished the season on the starting five.

I went out for football in the fall of 1955, my junior year, but got a job at the IGA grocery store and had to quit football due to the job. Coach wasn't happy and said I wouldn't be considered for basketball. I tried out anyway for basketball and won a position on the senior team as number ten of the eleven-player team.

It was a great basketball year, as I was able to work at the IGA and make arrangements to practice and play. But we had a mediocre season.

That was the last of my sports activities in high school. I sorely missed those activities, but earning a living was more important. I proved I could persevere and do more than most.

That was the last of my sports
activities...earning a living
was more important.

CHAPTER THIRTEEN

Working at the IGA Grocery Store

AS THE END OF my junior year approached, I was again trying to find some type of summer work. I still had the farm hay-making option, same as last year, in Trout Creek and Painesville, but I wanted to find a more stable job. Out of the blue, a classmate, John Doyle, approached me to ask if I was interested in working at the local IGA Grocery Store. He had been working there and decided that he was going to quit. The manager had asked him to recommend someone.

My reply: "Are you kidding? Yes, YES."

John took me to meet Jerry Hoefferle, the store manager, an ex-FBI agent who had been called home to run the IGA after his father suffered a heart attack. I was interviewed by the father, Mr. Hoefferle; the son, Jerry; the store manager, and another son, George, who was the store butcher. They were very thorough and wanted to know all about my background. They left me alone for a few minutes. Upon returning, Jerry said, "We'll let you know our decision in a week."

I spent the entire week praying that I would be hired. A week later, I received a call at my aunt's house, asking me to come back in. I was hired on a two-week trial basis and started working on the following Monday. I was in the eleventh grade, and I believe I started the trial job in May 1956. Since I was still in school, my work hours were from four o'clock to six o'clock after school Monday through Wednesday, and four o'clock to nine o'clock Thursday and Friday nights. Saturday hours began at eight o'clock in the morning and ran until six o'clock. The pay was fifty cents per hour (a whole twelve dollars per week). At the end of the two-week trial, I was called into Jerry's office and told I was hired as a regular store employee. Oh, I was so happy and relieved! I could now plan on working until the school year ended and then all summer between my junior and senior years. The summer pay would be fifteen dollars per week and I would work all the time the store was open. I could then work the school-year schedule through my senior year.

Oh, I was so happy and relieved! Now I had the stability I'd never felt before. What a windfall. I immediately found John and thanked him for giving me this opportunity.

I knew this job wouldn't be sufficient to permit me to begin thinking about college, but it was a start.

This job experience was fantastic. I was steadily given more and more responsibility. Soon I was in charge of ordering and stocking all the canned and boxed goods. I was regularly assigned to the meat department, and often took care of produce. When the check-out was busy, I would rush to assist, packing customers' groceries and carrying them to their cars. In time, Jerry even had me operate the cash register and check out customers' groceries.

I had the opportunity to meet so many new people and occasionally deal with the ones who weren't nice. More opportunities to expand my skills.

After working through the summer of 1956 and my senior year of high school, I needed to advise Jerry Hoefferle that I would be quitting upon graduation. This was a very difficult decision. I so enjoyed working in the grocery store and for the Hoefferle family. I decided to provide a proper two-week notice when I told Jerry I was going to leave and work that summer on a railroad section gang at the local pulp mill.

I think he realized I had a better-paying job, and he knew I was going to college. He invited me to lunch and said his brother George would also be coming. At the lunch, they offered me the following: if I went to Ohio to attend a meat- cutting school, they would pay all expenses, and upon successful completion, assign me to their new Ewen IGA as store manager. A real opportunity.

I thanked them for this generous offer and tried very carefully to use the right words to say, "I've been awarded a four-year scholarship for tuition and books at Michigan Tech in Houghton, and also have been academically accepted at General Motors Institute in Flint. I'm waiting to see if I can be hired by a GM Division, which is a requirement to go to this cooperative university. I really want to be an engineer of some type, as I so enjoy math and science."

They wanted to know more about these opportunities and they sincerely encouraged me, thanked me for my work ethic, and wished me well. They said, "You always have a job with us."

John Doyle remained in the Ontonagon and married his school sweetheart. We kept in contact over the years and even met in Ohio when he and his wife came to visit their children. John has been one of the leaders of our high school reunions, and my wife and I have attended almost all of them. A true friend!

CHAPTER FOURTEEN

Working at the Sinclair Service Station

IN THE SUMMER of 1956, while working at the IGA Grocery Store, I told the lady who supervised the produce department that I needed to earn additional money. She did an outstanding job at the store and had coached me on the many ways to enhance the sale of produce. She said her friend owned the Sinclair Service Station and had recently mentioned he was looking for someone to operate the station, so he could have time off. George Heinz evidently didn't have family to help. I asked her to give him my name.

A couple of days later, she said I should go and see George. Our meeting was very positive. George said he would have me work for about a week or so, to see if I would be suitable. The station was open every day from eight o'clock in the morning until nine o'clock at night, and he didn't have anyone else working.

My initiation period was set for the next week, from six to nine o'clock at night on Monday, Tuesday, and Wednesday. This wouldn't interfere with my work at the IGA, and if I got the job, it certainly would give me more knowledge and experience with cars and trucks.

The Sinclair Service Station was at the intersection of five roads and streets in Ontonagon, including the northern termination of US-45. It was a prime intersection, as all traffic of M-64 to the Porcupine Mountains from the southern and eastern parts of Michigan passed through this intersection.

The work was so different and interesting. When a car pulled up to the gas pumps, a bell sounded when the rubber tube was compressed by the car tires. I first asked the driver what he wanted, and, if it was gas, whether regular or premium.

Next, I asked how many gallons or dollars they wanted, and if I should check the oil. If a fill-up was requested, the goal was to complete cleaning the windshield before the pump automatically shut off. The bugs in the U.P. in the spring and summer are very prolific, so washing the windshield was a real chore. It was difficult to keep a smile when the driver or passenger pointed to the spots I missed.

George was a stickler for service, and he watched me carefully during my initiation period. If an oil check was requested, I had a shop rag in my back pocket ready to use. Removing the dip stick and wiping it clean was step one. Returning it, with a pause to permit the oil to attach to the dip stick, was the next step, and absolutely necessary. Upon removal, the dip stick must be shown to the customer for approval or deciding if additional oil is required. If additional oil was added, I showed the customer the new level for final approval. This was a way of confirming to the customer that the correct amount of oil was added.

The money was then collected. There were no credit cards in those days, and George only had a couple of customers using a credit account at the station. George had a system to enter the sale and then open the cash drawer, make change if required, and return the change to the customer. Each day the record and cash were to be reconciled, to be certain there wasn't a shortage of cash. George told me, "Any shortage of cash will come out of your paycheck."

As I recall, at the end of the first week, nine hours in all, George said I did a good job, and I was to come in on the next Sunday, to work from opening to closing (thirteen hours) with him. He wanted to show me more duties and give me some challenges to see how I would respond.

That weekend he showed me how to safely use the lift to raise the car for an oil change, and how to use tools for fixing flat tires. At the end of that Sunday, he said, "You're hired." My pay was seventy-five cents per hour, paid weekly. Oh, happy day! This was triple what I was making at the grocery store. I was so proud of myself.

Working for George was a great job. Soon I was also responsible to close out the cash drawer and verify that the total money remaining was correct. I don't ever recall any shortages requiring my pay being reduced.

All the challenges were new and exciting. Soon I was given a key for opening and closing the station on Sundays, and for putting the cash in the safe. I got to know many of the local people in town. On Sundays, older gentlemen would come to the station and sit and talk about old times or the latest gossip of the town. The Michigan State Police would stop on a regular basis for fuel and sometimes even require some sort of service.

I repaired car and truck tires, balanced wheels, aligned headlights, completed oil changes, and even replaced mufflers and tail pipes. After I purchased my forty-dollar Ford, George allowed me to use the station equipment when I had free time.

I continued to work all the same hours at the IGA, and then worked thirteen hours every Sunday at the service station until graduation. Later, when I was toting rail and gandy dancing, I continued the Sunday hours at the station, but also worked from six to nine o'clock on Thursdays, Fridays, and Saturdays. I did that until I left for college.

George was not only a great boss, but also became a very good friend. He encouraged me to continue my education and go to college. His dedication of serving the customer with honesty and integrity made an indelible impact on my life. I thank the Lord for the opportunity to work and learn from him.

CHAPTER FIFTEEN

The Accident

WHEN I WAS FIFTEEN, I left home permanently, after a final dispute with my abusive stepfather. I paid thirty dollars a month out of my thirty-five-dollar Social Security check to live with an aunt and her husband. Money was very tight, and I appreciated every dime I could earn. But in the fall of 1956, one of my goals was realized.

I bought a car.

During my senior year in Ontonagon, my friend Forrest Wiedbrauk sold me his 1942 Ford for forty dollars. I was the proud owner of a two-door, flat-head six-cylinder former military car.

Because the car was still war-time military green, it didn't take me more than a minute to decide to dress it up with a change of color. Of course, I could never afford to have it professionally painted. The important thing was, I owned a car, and the necessity of walking everywhere, including to work, was now going to be in my past.

My girlfriend was the sister of Forrest. Vera liked the idea of a paint job. "We can do it! Let's paint it by hand." She was always very sure of herself, with an infectious positive attitude, and kept encouraging me in many ways during those difficult years.

Vera and I went to the local Gamble's Hardware Store, where we found a close-out on several cans of farm equipment paint labeled "robin's egg blue." After buying the paint and a couple of better-quality brushes, Vera and I set to work painting the car.

We chose a few beautiful early fall days for the job, allowing drying time in between coats. What a huge project. It was almost impossible to eliminate the brush marks, but Vera was proficient at completing those finishing strokes with fewer brush marks, so I put the paint on and Vera finished the area. When we finally hit the open road, we quickly realized the car was visible for miles. The bright color also helped hide the brush marks. I actually believe Vera was happier and prouder than even I was.

For the previous three years, I had been working my way through high school without any family support, which necessitated that I earn an income. Since the day when I was seven years of age and my father died, I remembered the words an elderly neighbor told me: "Son, you are now the man of the family." I always tried to live up to that obligation, searching for work and earning money wherever I could find it: fishing, hunting, trapping, milking cows, driving tractors, chopping wood, and pulping. Now it was looking like my commitment was finally beginning to pay off.

In addition to the time required in high school, I was working at the IGA grocery store for two hours three nights a week, five hours on Thursday and Friday, and ten hours on Saturday, which amounted to twenty-four hours per week. On Sundays, I opened the Sinclair Service station at eight o'clock in the morning and closed it thirteen hours later. Another thirteen hours per week. In total, I was working thirty-seven hours per week in addition to attending high school.

Vera and her mother were waitresses at one of the three restaurants in town. They worked late into the evenings, serving dinners, and then cleaning up. With my schedule and Vera's late-evening schedule, we had little time to be together.

On that fateful Wednesday night, February 6, 1957, I picked Vera up at the restaurant a little after nine o'clock. Rather than immediately taking her home, we decided to take a short ride south of town.

It was just one of those seemingly never-ending cold, dark February winter nights in Ontonagon, with a slight wind coming off frozen Lake Superior. As we headed south of town on US-45, the wide black-topped road looked like an endless black pit. I was driving slowly, as the speed limit was twenty-five miles per hour and we had nowhere to go.

I was always very careful to avoid a costly ticket. The street lights, hanging over the center of the road, barely swinging, created shadows as the light reflected off the four-to-six-foot high snow banks covering the sidewalks.

Suddenly, out of nowhere, a small man wearing a long black winter coat staggered from the center of the road to the front of the car. "Where did he come from?" I gasped and swerved to the right. But the left side of the bumper, extending way out in front of the 1942 Ford, hit him in the legs, and he flew through the air.

I can still hear his scream.

I don't remember very much after hitting him, as I was probably in a state of shock. I remember the ambulance taking him away. I remember wondering if he was dead. I remember wondering what would happen to me. "Prison."

The police interrogated me to great lengths, and finally told me that I could go—for now. I was so upset I couldn't drive, so Vera drove my car to my aunt's house and her father came and got her.

The next days were a blur. I didn't know what to do, and I didn't have anyone to turn to for reliable or consolatory words. I learned the injured man was seventy-eight-year-old Joe Zupanic, someone I used to talk to when I walked to town. He was a nice old man, who was usually sitting on his porch when I passed by. We almost always had something to say to each other.

How could this have happened? Where did he come from? Why didn't I see him? Will he live? What will happen to me?

I had used my entire savings of forty dollars to purchase the car, so I had no money. What if I had to pay for the hospital? I should have bought the insurance! Can I ever drive again?

My nights were long and sleepless.

On the following Monday night, I heard a knock on the door at my aunt's house. There stood my friend Richard's father, Mr. Munro. He had been the prosecuting attorney for the county, but had lost in the last election. First, he told me the awful news. Joe had a broken arm, broken leg, and broken back. The doctors felt the old man may not make it — but if he did, he would need a very long time to recover.

I felt sick and stepped back to catch my breath, while saying to myself, "How will this end?"

Mr. Munro then said, "Let's not worry too much." He stepped forward and placed his hand on my shoulder, looking me in the eye, and continued, "I'm going to represent you."

I stammered, "I don't have money to pay you."

"I'm not going to charge you," Mr. Munro responded, "but I need you to do some investigative work to find details of what happened."

He had already discovered, on that frightful night, Joe had been drinking at a couple of bars and had left very drunk. Mr. Munro wanted me to find the bars and times Joe had been there, so the bar owners would know that I was collecting information, should there be any action against me. He further explained, "They definitely wouldn't answer me, an attorney, as we could possibly sue them for serving Joe when he was already drunk."

He also told me, "Social Security will pay the hospital bill. However, if there is negligence on your part, they'll sue for recovery of the money spent."

I thought I would faint at the word NEGLIGENCE. What else could happen? Does this ever end?

Mr. Munro turned to leave. "Do this investigation as soon as possible." But he turned back and looked me in the eye. "Let me know when you have the information."

I thanked Mr. Munro as I closed the door, and then immediately sat down for fear of falling.

The next day I began my investigation by going into the four bars I thought Joe might have visited. I found that he had spent the early part of the evening at Stubb's Bar. At the next two bars, I was told he wasn't there on that night. But when I questioned the couple at the Shamrock Bar, I ran into the first and only resistance. "It's none of your business," the owners simultaneously shouted, as they escorted me out of the bar.

I spent the next few days in a fog. I finally decided to go see Joe. I walked into his hospital ward, and when he saw me, he started to scream. "Don't kill me! Don't kill me!"

The nurses rushed into the ward and escorted me out of the room and hospital.

How can I ever live with this memory and feeling?

About two weeks after the accident, I was called out of class and told to report to the principal's office. When I walked into Mr. Webber's room, the local police chief was sitting there. Mr. Webber stood up and said, "The Chief has come to take you to a hearing before a judge. Pat, you must go." Mr. Webber was a big man, probably six-and -a-half-feet tall. He never smiled, he spoke very few words, and he was always very stern.

Fear was overcoming me. Mr. Webber also said, "Mr. Munro will meet you there."

I was still standing at attention when the Chief stood up and pulled out handcuffs. I frantically begged him, "Oh no, please, please no! Please don't walk me through school in handcuffs! I won't run."

All to no avail. I tried to hide my face as we walked, for what seemed forever, along the long hallway. The president of the high school Student Council was being walked out of school in handcuffs!

I didn't see anyone and never heard if anyone saw me. Of course, I never asked, but I was completely humiliated.

The Chief parked the car on the street, so anyone could see me being led in handcuffs into the building. I was placed in a room, still handcuffed, and told to wait. After some time, the Chief returned, removed the handcuffs, and escorted me into a large room where the judge sat behind a large desk.

I was seated next to Mr. Munro, who whispered, "Relax and answer only the questions you are asked." Mr. Munro did, on occasion, interrupt a question and objected that I didn't have to answer.

I don't remember any questions or discussions as I was in a state of shock. I was finally led, handcuffed, out of the big room and placed back in the original room. Did I answer the questions all right? Will I go to prison? The fear was overwhelming.

Time seemed to stop. A long time passed. Does this mean prison?

About forty-five minutes later, the Chief came and said, "You are free to go." He removed the handcuffs. Mr. Munro informed me the judge ruled there was no negligence on my part, and no criminal action would be taken. He also said that no records would be placed in my file concerning this matter.

Oh my gosh, the relief was unbelievable. I could breathe. I now knew God was watching over me.

Mr. Munro was also very happy and offered to take me back to school. I must have said "Thank you" a hundred times on our way back to school. I went right back to class, and no one said anything about the day or situation.

Joe did recover, but he was sent to a retirement home and I never saw him again. I thought this nightmare was over, but wrong again!

A couple of months later, I was stocking shelves at the IGA when a man I didn't know and didn't remember ever seeing, came up to me and said, "I know you're Patrick." He then confessed something that totally stunned me. "I've been living with terrible guilt. I want you to know, if you were charged by the police, I would've come forward and told my story."

"Your story!" I blurted out.

"I—I hit Joe with my car about ten minutes before you hit him. I didn't stop. I was scared."

I immediately went into that familiar state of shock, but now was very angry. How could this guy have done this, and kept his mouth shut? NOW ridding his guilt by telling me, after all this time! My anger overwhelmed me. I screamed at him, "Do you have any idea how I suffered? Do you think telling me will make YOU feel better? Why didn't you tell the police?" I threw off my apron and screamed, "Let's go and tell them, NOW."

He immediately drew back and shook his head. "I won't go to the police, and I'll deny we ever had this conversation. You only have my statement to go on." With that comment, he ran back to the entry door, found a way to open it, and I saw him running down the street.

It took a long time before I understood that I felt better. I realized that after he was hit, Joe had been lying on the black-top in his full-length black wool coat, and when he heard my car, he was trying to get up and out of the way. This is why he suddenly loomed into view, as he was staggering backwards toward the right side of the road. Possibly his broken bones caused the strange staggering. Maybe this was why my car was so close to the snowbank, on the right side of the road, when I stopped. I wasn't as much at fault as I had allowed myself to believe. Maybe, this was the answer that I needed, in order to be able to go forward and live with less guilt.

God had given me a wake-up call, heard loud and clear. I took a hard look at myself and my future, and started going back to church as much as possible. I also read the Bible more and renewed my strength after reading Romans 8:31, "If God is for you, who can be against you."

A verse I have never forgotten.

I may have had a hardscrabble life. I may have struggled to support my family and myself from a very early age. But Mr. Munro proved there are honest, caring people in the world. He continued to follow my journey through life, and we would often get together on visits with my family.

This experience proved that God truly was with, and for me, and I shouldn't fear adversity.

God had given me a wake-up call, heard loud and clear. I took a hard look at myself and my future and started going back to church.

CHAPTER 16

Toting Rail and Gandy Dancing

IN APRIL of 1957, just before my graduation from high school, I heard the local pulp mill might hire college students for the summer, to remove and replace the railroad tracks within the mill yard. I went to the pulp mill office to inquire and was informed that they might hire college students, but not young high school students. I decided this condition wasn't going to deter my efforts to get hired, if they did the project. I therefore embarked on a weekly trip to the mill office to ask about the job.

I said I was going to college and needed a summer job, so I wanted to be first on the list. On my third or fourth visit, the lady at the front desk asked me what college I was attending.

I responded, "Michigan Tech," even though I wasn't certain of it at that time. She, again said, "We may only be hiring college students who are already in college."

I responded, "How can I go to college, if I can't get a job? This decision to only hire someone already in college is not fair to me."

No response.

The next week I was there again. This time the lady left her desk even before I got through the door. The pulp mill manager came out of his office. He was a large tall man and walked with great authority. As he approached, he said, "I don't want to see you here anymore. You're becoming a nuisance."

I responded in the best tone and level I could muster, "I really need this job. If you hire, I want to be the first one."
I believe I struck the right nerve, because he stated, "If we hire students, you'll be the first one called."

I quickly responded, "How can you call since you don't have my phone number?"

He smiled and asked the lady to give me an application as he returned to his office. I quickly filled out the application and departed. I remember throwing arms in the air yelling, "YES!"

I was the first to be called. I started working on the railroad crew the first Monday in June 1957. I happily missed the last couple of days of school, of course after getting approval.

There were thirteen guys in this crew. We were to work eight hours per day, six days a week, and would be paid one dollar and fifty cents per hour. Wow, I was in the big time now.

Our foreman was an elderly guy, probably in his late fifties. He had worked on the railroad all his life and knew how to lay rail. Our first job was to pull up the old rail as the mill buildings were being revised. The incoming logs will be piled in different locations. Each rail was twenty feet long and weighed six hundred pounds. I was assigned, with three other guys, to carry the recently freed rails to areas adjacent to the new railroad grade locations. I remember how sore I was after the first few days.

Once the rails were moved, bulldozers made the new grade, near or on the old grade, with clay hauled in by trucks. It was necessary to survey and define a level surface for the new grade. The mill yard, with the new tracks, would have logs stacked on each side of the track. The loading and unloading of the logs required the track be level, so the train cars wouldn't roll to a different location while being unloaded or loaded.

The foreman called us together and asked if anyone knew trigonometry. I quickly raised my hand. I was totally surprised to be the only one, as I thought with all these college students, I certainly wouldn't be selected. So I was assigned to assist an engineer from the company. He told me he had never surveyed before, but with our combined knowledge and efforts, we figured out how to do it. It was fun—and I now had surveying in my bag of tricks.

Then the hard work started. We first hauled the new wooden railroad ties from a distant mill location and dropped them along the new grade. Once they were roughly in place, I was again assigned to help carry the steel rails to the new grade and place them on top of the new, loose, railroad ties.

I was next assigned to be a rail spike driver and given a ten-pound maul. My job was to drive railroad spikes into the railroad ties, to attach the steel rail to the wooden railroad tie. My assigned partner positioned a steel plate under the rail, between the rail and railroad tie, and lifted the tie up to the rail, using a long steel bar and block. A cantilever arrangement. I then drove a spike into the tie, on each side of the rail, attaching the rail to the tie. I swung that ten-pound maul forty-eight hours a week for about six weeks. I found myself sore, but developed the technique of swinging the maul to obtain the maximum driving force. We spike drivers were always competing to drive a spike with the least number of blows. A great way to build muscles and timing for an eighteen-year-old guy.

At the beginning, we certainly caused a problem, as we regularly broke off the heads of the mauls. The spike was very close to the rail, which is higher than the tie. Technique and skill were necessary for making the precision blow in order to avoid breaking the handle. The mill carpenter came to us shaking his head. "If anyone breaks one more handle, I'll come and break your arm." He said he was marking the handles, so he would know which guy's arm to break. From then on there were only a few handles broken.

After laying all the track, a train with tamp sand was brought in and released the sand from under the railcar, along the track, so it filled the track up to the top of the rail.

Now the gandy dancing began. The goal was to pack sand under the wooden railroad ties to change height and level the rails. We were assigned partners, and each partner was given a flat shovel. The process begins with the partners facing each other with the railroad tie between them. The shovels are simultaneously pushed down into the sand, immediately opposite each other. Each shovel handle is then simultaneously pivoted away from each other, using the top of the tie as the fulcrum point. The sand is pushed and packed under the tie. If this is continued, more sand is packed under the tie, and the tie and rail move upward.

The foreman used a level to guide us as we moved along the tie and tamped sand under it. We had to work in unison and do this while we were dancing on one foot. The other foot stayed on the shovel and attempting to push sand at each other at the same time. Singing a tune helped, but you can be assured that the sounds or songs weren't recordable.

Thus, the name Gandy Dancer.

We finished the railroad project ahead of schedule and were then assigned to clean up in the mill, because it was being expanded. All in all, it was a great summer. I was in the best physical shape of my life, and I made a significant amount of money for college.

A demonstration of the importance of persistence in accomplishing a goal.

I started working on the railroad
the first Monday in June 1957.
I happily missed the last
couple of days of school, with
permission, of course.

CHAPTER 17

College Bound!

WHEN I LEFT HOME at the age of fifteen to escape from my abusive stepfather, my only goal was survival. The thought of going to college was certainly not on the agenda. I needed to get away from the family farm before I did something I would regret for the rest of my life. To me, survival meant finding a place to live and earning enough money to sustain me until I could finish high school and come up with a new plan.

As graduation approached, my classmates were talking about their plans after high school. Quite a few were excited about going to college, while many of the guys were thinking about military service. I had worked constantly all summers since leaving home and forty hours per week all of my junior and senior high school years. I certainly didn't have any dreams of going to college—I knew I couldn't afford to go. I was just happy to make my first goal: graduating from high school.

And then one day, Mr. Webber, the stern and unsmiling high school principal, stopped and stunned me when he said, "Where do you plan to go to college?"

Shaken, I stepped back and without thinking, responded, "I don't think it's in the cards for me."

"That isn't true," he said sternly. "You should start thinking about where you want to go."

I indicated that I liked math and science and had thoughts about engineering.

A couple of weeks later, he stopped me in the hall and again asked, "What have you done about college?"

I remember feeling embarrassed, knowing I couldn't afford college. "Nothing," I said.

He handed me a brochure from Michigan Technology College of Mining and Engineering in Houghton. I thanked him, took it, and placed it in a textbook. Wow, someone is seriously interested in me and my future!

To my surprise, about a week later, Mr. Webber asked me, "What about college?"

"I read the brochure and would seriously consider Michigan Tech, but I can't afford it." I was embarrassed to be continually saying, "I can't afford it."

Without any hesitation he told me, "On your behalf, I've requested and received an application for a Michigan High School Scholarship. You should complete it."

What a surprise and shock! He went on to describe the scholarship. "If selected, the scholarship will cover tuition and books for four years, as long as the recipient maintains a B average."

What a fantastic opportunity. I was so excited I even thought I might hug him. He continued by saying, "Come to my office when you are free, to complete the application." At my first opportunity, I filled out the application, gave it to Mr. Webber, and thanked him so much I think he even thought about asking me to leave. But I really didn't think I had a chance.

A few days later, Mr. Webber approached me with a brochure for General Motors Institute in Flint, and explained he had received this brochure for many years, but no one ever investigated this college. I took the brochure, and found it very interesting, as it was a cooperative program, which I thought would be perfect for me. But, what chance would I have? Some U.P. kid going to a school operated by General Motors, one of the largest automotive corporations in the world?

Again, Mr. Webber had to press me to fill out the application. Finally, I did. To my surprise, I received a notice that I was academically accepted, but needed to be hired by a General Motors Division to become a student. A list of the divisions in America was provided, asking me to identify my first three choices if I applied.

All divisions in Michigan were on a four-week work period, followed by a four-week school period. Divisions outside of Michigan were on an eight-week work period followed by an eight-week school period. All students were on a year program with three weeks off in August and one week at Christmas.

I chose all three divisions in Flint. First, Fisher Body Division Flint No. 1, followed by Buick and Chevrolet. This decision meant I could live in one location for work and school.

As I look back at these decisions, I don't recall ever worrying about getting grades necessary to stay in the program.

In mid-May, I was informed that I had received the Michigan High School Scholarship at Michigan Tech and was accepted to start that fall. I was flabbergasted and overwhelmed. The word spread in school, and I received many congratulations.

Now what to do?

I hoped I could start with enough money to get through the first semester and maybe the first year. But what if I couldn't find a job next summer in the U.P.? I checked out future job possibilities, and I learned that few jobs were projected for next year. Mrs. Neuman, my math teacher, asked her husband, who was a manager in the Michigan Department of Transportation, about job opportunities for this summer and next year, and he told her they weren't hiring this year and most likely would not next year.

After just receiving the letter from Michigan Tech, I received a letter from Fisher Body Division, stating that student selection would be made from the results of aptitude tests held at the plant starting at eight o'clock on the morning of Monday, May 27. Dejected, I showed Mr. Webber the letter and explained, "I can't go. I don't have enough money. I used what I saved in preparation for graduation."

The next week, I was lying under my forty-dollar Ford trying to figure out if I could pull the transmission and repair it, as the first gear was blown. Someone came up to the car and asked, "Are you Patrick Winton? I'm from the Ontonagon Lions Club, and I'd like to talk to you."

I crawled out from under the car. To my surprise, he gave me a fifty-dollar check with my name on it from the Ontonagon Lions Club. "There is just one condition," he explained. "You must come to a Lions meeting and make a presentation of your experience taking the tests at Fisher Body and provide information about the General Motors Institute."

Wow! A gift like this for a parentless kid boarding in their town! All I could do was thank him and promise to give the presentation. I later found out that Mr. Webber was a Lion.

Two days before the scheduled tests, my girlfriend's father drove me the fifty miles to Baraga, where I boarded a Greyhound bus departing at midnight to Flint. I was very anxious and nervous as I boarded the bus. I had only been to Detroit when I was eight or nine years old.

Fourteen hours later, on a Sunday afternoon, I arrived in downtown Flint. I had no idea where the plant was located, so I hailed a cab. Based on the address, I was deposited on South Saginaw Street in front of the factory. There was nothing around except for a bar on the far corner opposite the factory, and other closed offices across the street. Oh, what do I do now? Where will I sleep?

Since I had spent thirty-two dollars for the bus ticket and five dollars for the taxi, I was fast running out of money, and I had no idea where I could find a place to stay for the night. I had no idea what to do.

I walked to the bar. On the corner of the building was a sign pointing to the back street, stating "Room by the day or week." I hurried to the narrow small house with the same sign and knocked on the door. An elderly lady came to the door and slightly opened it. I asked if she had a room for the night.

"No, we only rent by the week."

"But the sign reads, 'Room by the day or week.'"

She didn't give in.

In desperation, I continued, "Is there any place to stay the night? I have to be at the Fisher Body Plant tomorrow morning at eight o'clock, to take tests."

Her husband was evidently standing behind the door, listening, and he opened it so he could see me. "Where are you from and what are the tests for?"

I quickly responded, "I'm from Ontonagon in the U.P., and I've been invited to take tests tomorrow at the Fisher Body Plant. The tests will determine if I'm selected to go to GMI. It's my chance to go to college." I added that I had never been to Flint and had no idea where to sleep that night. They stepped away from the door, talked to each other, and then invited me to come into their house. After showing me the bedroom and bathroom, they wanted to know all about me.

Those people were so kind and supportive. They provided a wonderful dinner. The lady practically tucked me into bed. She woke me up early so I could shower, and she cooked a wonderful breakfast. They made certain that I was early for the walk to the plant and wished me luck, and they refused to take any money.

Another intervention by God's people.

I entered the factory to find about fifty guys in the lobby. Only two of us were wearing sport jackets. I had borrowed my girlfriend's brother-in-law's jacket, and I certainly felt out of place, but very happy I had made this effort. A number of guys asked where at General Motors my father worked. I quickly assumed you had to be a son of an employee to be considered.

We were escorted into a large room with long tables. The testing began promptly at eight o'clock. These timed tests covered all kinds of topics with strange questions, such as, "Do you take the stairs two at a time?" or "Do you find yourself walking in front of others?" All of which I normally experienced.

The testing went on for five hours. On the first test, I was the first to stand and present my answers. The other fellow with the sports jacket was second. This see-saw competition continued throughout the five hours, with only one ten-minute break. At one o'clock, we were finished. The man in charge asked the individuals from South Carolina and the U.P. of Michigan to stay for a tour of the factory. They also announced that the selection of students would be made later in the summer.

I met William (Bill) Shelnutt, the other guy wearing a sports coat, and Hal Hoelzal and George Walker, the coordinators of GMI students at Fisher Body No. 1. We toured the factory and were provided a nice lunch in the cafeteria. Bill suggested we catch a bus to GMI, and I gladly tagged along with someone that knew what he was doing in the big city.

My high school classmate Sally Bay had told me that her brother Jim had just been hired to teach at GMI. I had never met him, so I asked the GMI tour guide about him when we started the tour. We were taken to his office, introduced, and Jim gave us the tour. He wished us success and said he hoped he would see us at GMI. Bill had to catch his flight, so we had to leave. Bill got me on a bus to the Greyhound Bus Station, and he took a cab to the airport.

I had plenty of time to walk the streets of downtown Flint, eat some dinner, and wait for the midnight bus leaving for home.

Weeks went by. No word from Fisher Body. I wondered if I should call, but assumed I wasn't accepted. I made my presentation to the Lions Club, thanking them many times, but pointing out that I didn't know if I'd been accepted. I concluded that I would go to Michigan Tech, which meant I needed to save more money, since my Social Security benefit ended when I turned eighteen on May 29.

I was co-renting a shack on Lake Superior with a classmate who had taken a job as a local EMT. He worked nights and I worked days, so we didn't see each other very often. I ate meals at the restaurant where my girlfriend worked. The owner of the restaurant liked me and gave me specials at half price. Of course, I think she gave me the full portion.

One day in early August, I was told I had mail at my aunt's house. I was afraid to open the envelope, but, "Oh, Happy Day!" I read that I'd been accepted as an employee of Fisher Body Flint No.1, and was to report on Monday, September 23,1957. I would have one week of work before starting my first four weeks of school on September 30.

I informed Mr. Webber that I wouldn't be going to Michigan Tech. He said I must write a letter stating why, so the next person in line would be eligible for the scholarship.

The next challenge was to find a ride. Fortunately, Aunt Linda Bessen, my mother's sister, and her husband John said they wanted to go to Detroit and I could ride with them if I drove their car to Flint. They would then drive to Detroit.

I consolidated all my cash. I had saved a thousand dollars in my savings account and had some cash. When getting my belongings from Aunt Esther's, she asked me, "How can you afford to be going to college? You don't have any money."

This question startled me. "I've saved a thousand dollars," I said. She didn't believe me and demanded to see my savings book. As she looked at the number she said, "There is no way you could have that much money. From whom did you steal it?"

Without a response, I merely picked up my things and left. I now knew where I really stood with her.

Aunt Linda and Uncle John wanted to arrive in Flint in the morning, so they would have daylight to drive to Detroit, and I needed to arrive on Friday the 20th, so I could find a room to live in. We left on Thursday evening, September 19, as it would take about fifteen hours for the drive. We had to take the ferry across the Mackinac Straits, as the bridge wasn't yet completed.

We arrived in Flint around noon on September 20. GMI had a list of rooms for rent, and they would assist me to find a place to live. I stopped the car at the corner of Chevrolet and Third, got out of the car, grabbed my two small bags and watched the car drive away. I had all my worldly possessions and savings as I stood in middle of street, alone, wondering where I would sleep that night.

I walked into GMI, trusting that they would help me. So many good people, sent by God, to intervene in this phase of my life journey.

I grabbed my two small bags and watched the car drive away. I had all my worldly possessions and savings as I stood in the middle of the street, alone.

CHAPTER EIGHTEEN

First Years at GMI

ON FRIDAY AFTERNOON, September 20, 1957, I entered the Student Administration Office at the General Motors Institute to register and find a place to live.

I had to be at Fisher Body Plant 1 on Monday, September 23. The official school registration would take place on September 30, when all the new students arrived.

Everyone was very nice and gave me a list of people who would rent a room to GMI students. They also gave me a map, showing the location of each of the houses. I already knew I would have to use the Flint bus system to get to and from work at the Fisher Body Plant No. 1, located on South Saginaw Street, the main North/South Street in Flint.

When I was in Flint in May to take the tests at Fisher Body and visit GMI, I rode the bus from GMI to downtown. With this experience, I decided to look for places near Third Avenue, as this bus would also take me downtown, where I would transfer to another bus going to the factory.

I selected a house that looked in good shape, about one block from a bus stop on Third Avenue, and knocked on the door. When an elderly lady came to the door, I introduced myself and asked if she had a room for rent. She said she did, but only would provide a room if she had the opportunity to interview me and determine if I was fit to stay.

She wanted to know what section I was in, as she normally had C and D section students (eight weeks at school). I told her I was an A section student and would be staying all year, since I would be going to school and working while living in the same location. Her reaction was positive. I could sense she was interested. She wanted to know more information about where I was from, my age, and my family.

She said I would be able to keep some things in the refrigerator, but I couldn't cook. I also had to be quiet and not have friends over unless she approved ahead of time. The rental rate was seven dollars per week, and I was to pay two weeks in advance. She expected payment on time and any delay would mean I was to leave immediately. She had a special connection with GMI, and she would report me if I violated her rules.

I asked to stay that Friday night and informed her I was to report to Fisher Body on Monday, September 23. I would be working one week before starting school on September 30. I paid for two weeks, and she showed me to my room. She only had two bedrooms. The other renter (unfortunately I don't recall his name) had one more week of school before he went back to Columbus, Ohio. He would be on his eight-week work period, and I would be the only one here for the next eight weeks.

The next day, Saturday, I checked the bus schedule to downtown and the transfer bus to the factory. I decided to take the buses and evaluate the return schedule. I felt confident that I was going to be okay using the bus for transportation, as I could be at the plant early and could easily catch a bus back without rushing from work. I would be walking to school, as it was only a fifteen-minute walk. On Monday, September 23, 1957, I was dressed and ready for my first day at Fisher Body. In my normal style of always being early, I was there before the office even opened. I had to wait outside on the sidewalk, as the guard refused to let me pass.

Upon entering, I was escorted to the coordinators' office, where I met the two gentlemen who had officiated at the tests, Hal Hoezal, and George Walker.

The starting pay was two dollars and thirty-two cents per hour. I was informed I could have started working immediately after receiving the acceptance letter. What a bummer, as I could have worked at least a whole month and increased my income in August. I was very upset to think of all the money left on the table.

I also found out that only two students were accepted from all those tested. Bill from South Carolina and me. I worked the normal forty-hour week and then started my four weeks of school.

The normal school class load was twenty-five to twenty-seven credit hours per semester. Classes were held from eight o'clock in the morning to five o'clock at night, Monday through Friday, and eight o'clock to noon Saturday. The school was closed for one week at Christmas and three weeks in August. Whenever possible, I arranged to work during these breaks, to earn extra money.

As I recall, my first semester tuition was four hundred and fifty dollars, in addition to at least two hundred and fifty dollars for books. The books were very expensive, and I tried to buy as many used books as possible. So, with this original outlay of cash, my savings were depleted so much that I was very worried about paying the next semester's tuition and books. I was careful with my money and only ate dinner at a local restaurant, where I was able to get a half portion for half the price.

Alas, at the end of the first semester, I was out of money after paying for tuition and books for the second semester. I was desperate and felt I was done and would have to quit. No money for food, and my clothes certainly weren't nearly as nice as other students'.

The first event that helped was when I told a friend, Bob Wimmer, who also ate at the Copper Kettle Restaurant, about running out of money. Another guy who was often in the restaurant overheard me and wanted to know more. After I explained my situation, he quietly said he delivered institutional food to restaurants and other facilities and he would sell me a case (twenty-four cans) of Spam for a dollar.

I agreed, and I walked home with a case of Spam. I still had about two weeks of school and then had to work one week before receiving a check at the end of the second week. I ate Spam and soda crackers for those four weeks. When the landlady knew of my situation, she let me boil, broil, and fry the Spam. Water, soda crackers, and Spam become very boring if you eat them for breakfast, lunch and dinner.

When I arrived at the plant for my next work period, I went to the coordinator, Mr. Hoezal, and told him of my dilemma, that I needed to have more income or I would be forced to quit at the end of my first year at GMI.

Immediately, he made a few phone calls, and I was assigned to a job that required twelve hours per day, five days per week. Fisher Body Flint No. 1 manufactured and shipped all the Buick bodies for Buick cars directly to the Buick Motor Division Plant also in Flint. Buick station wagon bodies designed by Fisher Body were assembled using parts supplied by a company in Owosso and shipped directly to Buick. Fisher Body employees worked at the Buick factory, inspecting and finishing the station wagon bodies before releasing them to Buick.

My assignment was to be available at the Buick plant to return or pick up parts from Fisher Body Plant No.1, so the station wagon bodies could be completed. I was given a brand new 1958 Buick Electra 225 car, and waited in it for orders from the station wagon assembly supervisor. I immediately drove the seven miles to the Fisher Plant and returned to Buick with the parts needed. I often made more than six trips per twelve-hour shift and also had the experience of getting extra sleep while waiting.

These additional hours, paid time-and-a-half, meant my weekly pay increased from ninety-three dollars to one hundred sixty-three dollars. I worked the whole month on that schedule, and to my surprise and thankfulness, the job continued for one year.

When I returned to school, I approached the Student Relations Office to ask if I could apply for a job during the school period.

They sent me down to the athletic club, where I met the manager. It so happened that he was originally from Ontonagon County, only a few miles from the family farm. He hired me to work a couple of hours in the evenings and each Saturday when I was free from classes. I checked sports equipment throughout my remaining time at GMI.

Near the end of my first year, I decided I could improve my situation and income if I rented a house, or part thereof, and sub-rented rooms to other guys when they came to school or to work. Some were in fraternities during the school period, but weren't permitted to stay there during their work periods. I subsequently rented the downstairs of a house with three bedrooms, located on the corner of 11th Avenue and Lyon Street, and sub-rented to my friends. They always had a place to stay whenever they came to town.

My agreement with the house owner, in addition to monthly rent, was to cut the grass and shovel the snow. There were two apartments upstairs, and they were rented to non-GM people. I had no responsibility for them.

My other major hurtle came to a head in my second year.

My teeth had steadily deteriorated, and I was faced with constant toothaches. All the old fillings were falling out, and I was in terrible pain. I finally had to do something when I had three abscessed teeth. My face was swollen and I wasn't able to concentrate on my school work.

Bob Wimmer and his wife Shirley recommended their dentist, and I went to see him. At the first appointment, he informed me that the best thing to do was to have all my upper teeth removed, some of the lower teeth pulled, and a full upper plate and a partial plate made for the bottom. He told me what this would cost. I didn't faint, but I thought I would. It was more money than I could possibly pull together.

I told him that I could pay him a fifty-dollar deposit that day and so much per month. He said he didn't accept credit accounts and I should come back when I could guarantee payment. I remember asking if I could at least have the abscessed teeth removed. He asked what I would do if only this was done. I told him I would have to quit school and see if I could join the service, as they might fix my teeth.

He said he didn't think they would take me into the service with teeth like mine. About this time, his wife, the assistant, came into the room. She undoubtedly had been listening and asked to talk to her husband. They left the room. When he came back, he said that they had agreed to take the risk of allowing me to pay the bill over time. I could now pay fifty dollars to start, and twenty-five dollars per month, more if possible. We filled out paperwork, and he started the process that day. I had to clear up the infection before some of the teeth could be pulled.

The dentist planned to pull all my upper and lower back teeth and then make the full upper and partial lower plates. When the plates were ready, the front teeth (the few I had left) would be pulled and the upper plate would be inserted at the same time. "This might be uncomfortable," he said, but he told me I would be guaranteed a better fit, since I would have a full upper plate for the rest of my life.

As I reflect back, it seems this procedure made when I was nineteen entirely changed my life. I stepped out from the past and into the future.

Alas, at the end of the first semester, I was out of money... I was desperate and felt I was done and would have to quit.

CHAPTER NINETEEN

GMI and Family

IN JANUARY of 1958, just as I began the second semester of my first year at GMI, I received a letter from my thirty-nine-year-old mother, telling me that my new half-brother, Benjamin Kaare, had died the day after his birth. It was quite a shock to me, as I hadn't been aware that my mother was pregnant. She went on to say that her heart problems had become more acute, and she had to make a decision about what to do. She wanted my input.

My mother had been suffering from many health issues during the years I was on the family farm, starting in 1953. By the time I left the farm in September 1954, she couldn't even walk to the barn without stopping a couple of times. She told me she was unable to breathe and her heart was pumping very fast. The doctors had now diagnosed her problem to be a defective mitral valve as a result of having rheumatic fever when she was a child. They estimated that her mitral valve opening, normally the size of a quarter, was only the size of a pencil tip and it wasn't closing as it should, due to scar tissue. They said she only had three months to live without surgery and a fifty/fifty chance of surviving radical open heart surgery. Mother was asking for my opinion as to what she should do.

Oh, I was so surprised with all this news and immediately felt so guilty for being so engrossed in my own issues. I asked myself what I could and should do and say.

I couldn't call home as they didn't have phone service in the area at that time. I can't recall what I said in my return letter, but her next letter stated she was going to have the surgery on May 30, in Duluth, Minnesota. She made a special request that I be there before she went into surgery. I started to plan on how I would travel from Flint to Duluth, and asked a number of people for ideas. I had developed a friendship with Jim Bay, the GMI professor who was the brother of my high school classmate. Jim said that he and his family were going to Iowa for the Memorial Day weekend and I could ride with them to Dubuque. Jim and his wife, originally from Iowa, found out there was a train from Dubuque to Duluth via Minneapolis.

We decided to depart on May 28. I would catch the train that evening in Dubuque for an overnight ride to Duluth, arriving on May 29, the day before Mother's surgery.

I would be able, on the return, to catch a train from Duluth to Dubuque on June 1 and meet them for a ride back to Flint.

The drive to Dubuque and the train connection went exactly as planned. On the leg from Minneapolis to Duluth, I was seated facing a couple returning to Duluth. They were particularly interested in why I was traveling by myself. After divulging the purpose of my trip, they asked, what hospital my mother was in.

"I don't know. Is there more than one?" I asked.

Upon arrival in Duluth on the morning of May 29, the couple accompanied me to a phone booth. I called one hospital and learned mother was not a patient there. The only other hospital was St. Mary's, and the phone call confirmed Mother was there.

The couple drove me to St. Mary's, stopped at the front entrance, and said they would be praying for my mother. The receptionist directed me to the floor and room number. Leaving the elevator and walking down a long hall, I was suddenly met by my stepfather, George, who was leaving a waiting room. He was crying. When he recognized me, he grabbed me in a bear hug, while sobbing so hard he was unable to speak.

A nurse came running toward us. From a distance, she shouted loudly, "Are you Pat?" When I responded, "Yes," she grabbed my arm and pulled me forward. "Come! Hurry! We aren't able to get a blood pressure reading." We raced down the hall and entered a long narrow room. Mother's bed was at the far end, and a nurse was sitting next to her. When Mother said, "Pat," the nurse gasped, jumped up, and ran toward us. In surprise, I quickly moved next to Mother and grabbed her out-stretched hand. "What is happening? The surgery is tomorrow. What's wrong?"

Before I could say anything to her, a team of people rushed into the room, and I was escorted out. My sister Trish rushed to me and grabbed me in a hug. "They did the surgery yesterday," she said, "and Mother hasn't responded since. Your entrance must have shocked Mother out of her non-responsive state. Her blood pressure has returned."

I learned that Mother's heart was removed from her body and the mitral valve opening was so small that she wouldn't have lived more than a couple of weeks. The valve was reworked by slicing and removing the scar tissue so the valve would open and close properly, as originally designed by God. This open-heart surgery took place in 1958, very early in mitral valve surgery history.

Mother's original reworked valve continued to work for the next thirty years. She only needed a replacement in the late 1980's. One tough lady.

As May, 29, 1958 was coming to an end, I started to think about where I might spend the night. Trish said she was going to sleep in Mother's room, where George had stayed the last couple of nights. All three of us had a dinner at the hospital cafeteria. George said he previously stayed at the YMCA next door to the hospital. He and I walked there and requested two rooms. Suddenly being with George was, for me, like walking on egg shells, as we hadn't been together since the incident on August 1954, four years earlier.

The young man behind the YMCA counter broke the spell by saying, "We are fully booked tonight. I only have one room. I can get you another cot, if you two are able to stay in the last room." Oh my gosh, I was immediately scared and didn't know what I was going to do. George looked at me and said, "I am fine sleeping in the same room as you."

I know I hesitated, but finally said, "I'm also okay."

We were shown to a very small YMCA room and the other cot was brought in. I made certain to arrange the cots so our feet were in a corner and our heads as far apart as possible. Fine with me. My head was close to the door, and I could make a fast exit if necessary.

I recall dozing off, but woke suddenly when I heard George crying. "Are you okay?" I asked.

"No, I'm so worried about losing your mother, I haven't slept for some time." Our conversation moved from Mother's present condition to the death of Benjamin, the birth of my half-sister Linda in October of 1955, and Trish's decision to leave home when she started the tenth grade. She went to live with our Aunt Ethel, our dad's sister, who lived in Iron River.

To my amazement, George said he was sorry for what he had done to me. The rage in me began to rise. Also my voice. I wanted to scream. I couldn't believe what I was hearing. The years of hatred were beginning to take over. But for some unexplainable reason, I began to calm down. We talked about the past and how we had hurt each other with words and deeds. We agreed to do our best to reconcile our past and do this for the sake of Mother. Then we prayed together.

God certainly was at work that night.

We spent family time together on May 30 and 31. No one, not even I, remembered that my nineteenth birthday had been the day before, May 29th.

I had to depart on the train on the evening of the 31st. The trip was an overnight to Dubuque to meet the Bay family for the ride back to Flint. Mother's condition was improving, so I departed relatively confident of her recovery, and maybe the family's.

George and I experienced a change in our relationship and how we dealt with each other. It wasn't easy, but the efforts continually improved until the day he passed. I'm certain that the improved relationship helped Mother begin to live a long and relatively comfortable life.

Another important thing happened about that time. Just before I went to Duluth, my friend and renter, Mitch Marchi, and his girlfriend, Janie, had convinced me to go on a blind date with Janie's girlfriend. After a lot of begging, I finally agreed. I didn't have a car, I didn't have any nice clothes, but I did have fake front teeth and others that were rotting. I also had no extra money. Mitch said we could ride with them to a drive-in movie. "Don't worry."

As we drove to my date's house, I thought I would refuse to go in, but I found the courage to knock on the front door.

A young girl opened the door. As I stepped into the living room, I was facing five girls and parents. I immediately saw the smiling, beautiful blond girl standing in the middle, of the crowd and hoped she was Elaine. She was. And my world changed.

Neither one of us could ever remember what movie we saw, because we talked throughout the movie. The evening was wonderful. I saw her again a couple of times before l went to Duluth and learned that her old flame, now in the Army, was returning while I was in Duluth. I'll admit I was very concerned that I would soon be forgotten. But when I returned, I found that this didn't happen. We continued to develop our relationship throughout the next three years before I finally asked her to marry me.

In the second semester of my junior year, the personnel director of Fisher Body Plant asked if I was interested in being interviewed for a transfer to the Fisher Product Service Department at the headquarters in Warren, Michigan. I didn't even have to think about taking this opportunity. I immediately accepted. I was interviewed, selected, and started working in this operation in my junior year. I was very proud of this opportunity, as I never heard of a student transferring between operations.

I worked in all the various activities of Product Service and was selected to do my Fifth Year Project studying and recommending solutions for historical warranty service problems. Upon the successful conclusion of the Fifth Year Project, I was assigned as a Service Engineer, responsible for writing service manuals and service bulletins for car dealers to take care of service issues on General Motors automobile car bodies.

After completing my Fifth Year Project, I was awarded a Bachelor of Mechanical Engineering Degree from GMI.

While working in Product Service, I became acquainted with the director of salaried personnel in the headquarters of Fisher Body, a facility with about three thousand employees. I unofficially inquired about opportunities for engineering work in other areas at the headquarters. He informed me there were official protocols that must be followed for this to occur, and I should talk to my supervisor.

I told him that I couldn't do that, as I would certainly limit my opportunities by showing my desire to leave the department.

To my surprise, a few weeks later, I was called into my supervisor's office and informed that Manufacturing Development Activity was interested in interviewing me for an engineering position. My supervisor looked me straight in the eye and asked if I was aware of this interest. I answered I didn't even know of this operation and had no idea how this could have occurred.

I was interviewed by the director of manufacturing development, the engineer-in-charge, and a supervisor, and learned there were ten GMI graduates in the department and they all had spent their four years working there and writing their Fifth Year Projects. "Does this competition bother you? You'll be competing against them for any advancements."

I remember my quick response was, "I'm not afraid of any competition and will look forward to it. I want to be the best I'm capable of."

A week later, the director of salaried personnel came to Product Service and requested I meet with him and my supervisor. The announcement was made that I would be transferring to Manufacturing Development activities. This proved to be best move I made in my fifteen-year career with the Fisher Body division of the General Motors Corporation.

CHAPTER 20

In Conclusion

BY THE END of my second year at GMI, I had overcome many of my past limitations. By the end of my Fifth Year Project, I received a Bachelor of Mechanical Engineering degree from one of the best engineering schools in the United States. I was also able to graduate as a member of the honorary engineering fraternity Alpha Tau Iota.

After four years of night classes at Wayne State University, I was rewarded with a Master of Science in Mechanical Engineering Degree. And, even better, I began visiting my mother and stepfather, and we reestablished a family relationship that included my sisters Trisha and Linda, as well as my brother Joe, the baby Trish and I had cared for at such a young age.

My most important and significant event was meeting Elaine, my loving wife and inspiration. She is my true partner, the mother of our three children. I was no longer alone in the world without a family.

I thank God for walking with me and opening all these doors and opportunities. I don't think I would be writing these words if it had not been for God's leadership. At times when I most needed help, encouragement, and direction, God placed special people to help me along the way. I've always said, "People made the difference in my life."

The early hardships and deprivations in my life truly prepared for a future that would bring me so many opportunities—all the result of being farmed out.

My mother's parents, Kreeta and Antti Hietala, both immigrated from Finland at the turn of the last century. According to the family story, my grandfather had been a Russian soldier. They met in Michigan, married in Ishpeming, and homesteaded in Ontonagon County on eighty acres.

After settling into our new little house, Mother began suffering severe back difficulties. She was sent to the Ontonagon Hospital on many occasions, and she would be gone for days each time. This situation continually created challenges for us all: where we could live and who would care for Trish, my beautiful blond sister, and me.

Our farming-out days began.

When I left home at the age
of fifteen to escape my
abusive stepfather, my only
goal was survival.

When I left home at the age of fifteen to escape my abusive stepfather, my only goal was survival.

When someone would start singing 'All I Want For Christmas Is My Two Front Teeth,' all I could do was to increase my grade point average and work harder.

ABOUT THE AUTHOR

"You're the man of the house now, Pat."

After learning that Pat Winton's father had dropped dead, a neighbor outlined the course of the seven-year-old's future. From that moment in 1946 onwards, heavy burdens fell on the boy's skinny shoulders. He tried to help support his mother and younger sister on a rural Finnish homestead in Michigan's Upper Peninsula.

He struggled just to survive. But, thanks to hard work, perseverance, and a firm belief in mankind's better nature, he learned not only how to survive, but also thrive.

After earning scholarships and a degree from the General Motors Institute, his early career focused on the auto industry and raising a family with his wife Elaine. He earned a master's degree in mechanical engineering, and in time became co-owner of an international company producing automated machines for producing small electric motors. During those years, he wrote and published technical papers and patents, always intending one day to tell a more personal story.

In retirement, his life took an entirely different tack. Pat transformed a boating hobby into a retirement challenge. After earning his USCG Captain's license, he and Elaine led boating getaways and moved new yachts on adventures throughout the Great Lakes, the Mississippi River, the Pacific, and the Atlantic Eastern Seaboard.

When Elaine's health began failing, Pat accepted yet another challenge at the age of eighty-two: creative writing. Since completing his coming-of-age memoir Farmed Out in Ontonagon County, Pat is hard at work on several new writing projects.

www.PatWinton.com